AMERICAN INDIAN IDENTITY:
TODAY'S CHANGING PERSPECTIVES

Edited By
Clifford E. Trafzer

Sierra Oaks Publishing Co.
1986

Printed in the United States of America

Library of Congress
Catalog Card Number
86-062561

This anthology first appeared in the series, San Diego State University Publications in American Indian Studies and is reprinted with the permission of the series editor.

CONTENTS

Preface

Two professors walked down the sidewalk together on their way to class. Autumn had arrived early, and the leaves on the maple trees had turned red and gold. The two teachers talked about a new colleague in their department, an American Indian. One of the professors was troubled that an Indian had "arrived" and had joined the faculty of his academic department, but he consoled himself with the belief that his new colleague had been appointed because he was an Indian, not because he was a fine teacher or scholar. He confided to his friend that the new member of the faculty should wear a feather, since that would help identify the person as the department's Indian. The feather would also separate this faculty member from others. The professor laughed and walked on to his class. He never accepted his new colleague, and he never believed that an American Indian belonged on his campus with the status of a university professor.

When most people think of American Indians, they think of feathers, horses, war whoops, and wampum. They rarely think of Indians as being university professors, teaching and writing about their own people. But times have changed and so have American Indians. Indeed, Indians have never been stagnant people, and individual Indians and their cultures continue to change today. The changes have been profound, affecting every aspect of American Indian life, from their clothing to their technologies. To address all aspects of this social and cultural phenomenon would be impossible, but an attempt is made here to examine a few elements of American Indian society as it relates to the question of identity. Several authors have contributed essays, and they hope that the ideas they have shared might yield additional thought and deeper scholarly interest.

The authors of these essays are Indians from various parts of the country who are closely associated with the Department of American Indian Studies at San Diego State University. All of them are specialists in the field of American Indian Studies, and most of them are scholars from a major university in the United States. With the exception of one person, all of them have been members of our faculty, and they have shared their ideas with our students through their lectures and their writings. This work is a collection of their thoughts and theses and will be used to supplement our departmental curriculum. Seven unique and original studies are published here, and the anthology constitutes the first in a series of scholarly publications presented by our department. The scholars who have contributed essays are thanked for researching and writing their works. To each of them, I express my sincere appreciation. Their interest in San Diego State University and the academic goals of the Department of American Indian Studies is deeply appreciated.

Several other people have made this publication possible. President Thomas Day and Vice-President Albert Johnson are thanked for their support of this departmental project. I also extend my gratitude to Dean Robert Detweiler and Associate Dean Marilyn Boxer for their kind support of our department and this publication. My appreciation is given to Geraldine Washabaugh and Linda Hammond for proof-reading the manuscript. Also, I extend my gratitude to Joe Renteria and Juti Winchester who saw the manuscript through the final stages of publication. Kathy Peck receives my sincere praise for managing our departmental office and for typing many drafts of this anthology.

I thank the Academic Council of the Department of American Indian Studies for their interest in our activities, particularly those scholars who served as referees for these essays. Furthermore, my appreciation is extended to Raymond Starr, Thomas Cox, Richard Griswold del Castillo, Bud McKanna, Ralph Forquera, Richard Scheuerman, David Stratton, Raymond Muse, and Larry Leach for their help and encouragement during the past three years. I thank the members of my extended family for their support, particularly Lee Ann who helped me in so many ways. Finally, I want to recognize the contribution of John C. Rouillard, the former chair of our Department. With the help of the community, students, staff, and faculty, he built our department. To John C. Rouillard and to the others, this first publication is gratefully dedicated.

Clifford E. Trafzer
March 1, 1985

Introduction

When Christopher Columbus first arrived in the Americas, he identified the peoples he met as Indians, believing that the inhabitants of the Carribean Islands were related to those of India's mainland. Of course, he was wrong, but the identification of Native Americans as Indians has stuck and typifies the ambiguity surrounding the American Indian identity. Thus, from first contact with Europeans, the question of an American Indian identity was raised. The issue remains to this day and is addressed in several different ways by the authors presented in this volume.

R. David Edmunds is a Professor of History at Texas Christian University and has provided an essay titled, "Antelope and the Engineers: Challenge and Change in the Indian Communities," which probes the issue of Indian "traditionalists" and "progressives" within the Indian communities of the United States. He illustrates the continuity between the past and the present, arguing that Indian societies and cultures have always been adaptive and that this is as true today as yesterday. Edmunds suggests that Indian tribes and peoples have the opportunity to grow in many different directions, and he suggests that the progressive path of formal education is one of the greatest avenues open to today's Indians. Professor Donald L. Fixico of the Department of History, University of Wisconsin, Milwaukee, has contributed, "From Indians to Cowboys: The Country Western Trend." He maintains that the Indian identity was altered by the westward movement and that many Indians have gravitated toward an identification with the larger Western American society. Fixico focuses on country western music, cowboy boots, broad-brimmed hats, and other items of dress as well as the importance of the media, rodeos, and horses.

Clifford E. Trafzer, Chair and Professor of American Indian Studies at San Diego State University, has written "The Twentieth Century Horse: The Role of the Pickup Truck in Indian Country." He examines the significant contribution of the pickup to Indians living in rural regions of the country today. He details the many functions of trucks for transportation and communication, and he demonstrates that for many Indians, the pickup has replaced the horse. Christopher Bentley has spent his life studying the material culture of the Plains Indians and has offered a portion of his research in his work, "The Comanche Shield: Symbol of Identity." Bentley suggests that the identity of Indians, in the past and present, was tied to natural elements of the universe used to make many ceremonial items. His example is the ceremonial shield of the Comanche, and he details the origin, construction, and use of this symbol of one tribe of the Great Plains.

Michelene Fixico is a Visiting Professor of American Indian Studies, San Diego State University, and has offered her essay, "The Road to Middle Class Indian America." In her comparative work she argues that while white college students in the 1960s and 1970s drifted away from the economic and social values of middle class America, Indian students gravitated to "traditional" Indian values. During this era, Indians emphasized the family and showed increased awareness of their identity as Indians. Professor Fixico argues that an Indian renaissance emerged out of the period, and she illustrates her thesis by examining the Indian takeover of the Bureau of Indian Affairs Building in Washington, D.C., and the Wounded Knee conflict of 1973. She concludes that while Indians have moved toward traditional values and beliefs, they have also attempted to reach a middle class existence by improving employment, education, and other measures of social and economic opportunity.

The last two essays deal with the Indian identity as it relates to professional scholars, particularly those associated with American Indian Studies Programs. Carol Hampton of the University of California, Berkeley, has contributed, "Tribal Esteem and the American Indian Historian." She examines two important issues facing American Indians who are professional scholars. First, Hampton points out that Indian historians have an intellectual obligation to enlighten and educate, using traditional scholarly sources as well as "Indian" sources, including written and oral accounts. However, Indian scholars have another obligation and that is to their people. As members of the American Indian community, elders often confide in young scholars, sharing knowledge which they considered to be the sole domain of the tribe, especially information of a religious and sacred nature. Hampton uses examples involving the Native American Church and the Caddo Tribe of Oklahoma to examine this problem.

Finally, Professor Carter Blue Clark, Chair of American Indian Studies at California State University, Long Beach, has presented, "America's First Discipline: American Indian Studies." Clark's chapter outlines the contributions of the field and intimates the problems that have beset the small academic units since their creation over a decade ago. He offers some perceptive insights in his work, largely based on his extensive experience in the field. Like the other authors, Clark is concerned with the question of identity and the challenges American Indian Studies Departments have faced in developing their unique place within the framework of non-Indian institutions of higher education.

AMERICAN INDIAN IDENTITY

Chapter 1

Antelope and the Engineers
Challenge and Change in the Indian Communities

by R. David Edmunds

October is a time of change on the wind-swept plains of northwestern New Mexico. On some days the dying summer lingers, but on others, when the first of the northern winds sweep down, long blue lines of storm clouds roll south, presaging the winter to come. On one such day a small village of short skin lodges clung to the base of a river bluff, seeking protection from the cold rain approaching across the northern horizon. In one of the lodges, two Kiowa men sat smoking long stemmed pipes before a small campfire. Although they were members of different clans, they had known each other since childhood, and their friendship had been strengthened by the years that their families had walked together, following the buffalo herds across the plains.

Antelope, the older of the two men, recently had returned from many days walk to the south, and he was eager to share his experiences with his friends. Excited by his discoveries, he told the younger man, Wolf-That-Follows, of a magnificent new animal he had seen near the Rio Grande. "The Jumanos, who dwell in mud houses, gave me food and took me to see strange hairy men with ash colored faces." Both men had previously heard of the strangers, but Antelope's description of their animals left Wolf-That-Follows incredulous.

"They have animals which the Jumanos call Medicine Dogs which stand as high as an elk, and although they have no antlers, they have hair upon the backs of their necks, and their tails are great masses of hair which hang down behind their legs like bunches of the tall grass that grows along the river valleys."

"Do they bark and warn the camp when strangers approach?" asked Wolf-That-Follows, who had lived all his life among the packs of dogs that skulked through Kiowa villages.

"No," replied his friend. "But they carry burdens just as our dogs do when the village moves, and what is more astonishing, they allow men to ride upon their backs, sitting behind their shoulders."

"Do they not turn and snarl at the riders and try to grab them with their teeth? Aren't the Jumanos afraid that these dogs will eat their children?"

Wolf-That-Follows had trouble comprehending such animals, and the thought of men riding upon them only compounded his amazement. "Did you touch these medicine dogs?" he asked. "Did the Jumanos place you upon the animals' shoulders?"

Turning his eyes away from his friend, Antelope first looked at the pipe cradled in his hand, then at the campfire. "They told me that the animals would carry me, but their medicine was too strong. I refused to approach them. Yet these great dogs have remained within my mind as I walked the many days back to our village. Now I wish that my courage had been greater, and that I had sat upon their backs when the Jumanos tied a rope around their neck and led them through the village."

Wolf-That-Follows remained skeptical. "My friend," he replied, "You were wise to shun these evil creatures. Dogs of that size undoubtedly hold a powerful medicine, and they might have harmed you in ways that are unknown to our people. Moreover, what good are the beasts to us? We have always followed the buffalo, and dogs of such size would frighten the herds and make the hunt more difficult. Such animals were unknown to our fathers and have no meaning in our lives. I believe we should follow the old ways. Our circle remains unbroken. That which was, is now. Our lives must remain the same."

But Antelope had a different vision. "What if we could bring these great dogs into our village? What if we could ride on their backs to hunt the buffalo? Why couldn't our women pack our possessions on their backs and lead them with ropes, like the Jumanos do in their villages. Surely these new beasts would transform our lives. Perhaps our path would be different from that of our fathers, but wouldn't it be better if we could use the beasts for our purposes?"

Wolf-That-Follows refused to be persuaded. "My friend," he replied, "We have always walked behind the buffalo herds. Our women and dogs have always carried our burdens. If we change, we lose the old ways. We betray our fathers." Then, looking at Antelope, he warned, "New ways and new ideas have no place around our campfires. Our future will be dark if we welcome the medicine dogs into our villages."

* * * * * *

Two centuries later, two Cherokee men sat beside a stone hearth in a log cabin in Georgia. Like Antelope and Wolf-That-Follows, they too were faced with accepting certain changes and new ideas which were available to their people. Approaching middle-age, Jonathan Westbrook was a half-blood whose name reflected his father's Scots-Irish lineage, but whose upbringing had been within the framework of a traditional Cherokee village.

His friend, Water Snake, was a full-blood who also had been raised in the village, but who had sporadically attended a mission school which had been opened near a trading post on the Coosa River.

Westbrook was worried about an event which recently had transpired among the Western Cherokees, those members of the tribe who lived across the Mississippi, in northern Arkansas. By 1820 Sequoyah, a mixed-blood residing in Arkansas, had compiled a syllabic alphabet of the Cherokee language, and the next year he returned to Georgia, spreading the knowledge of his new system of writing among his eastern kinsmen. Since that time, interest in the new learning had grown and many of the eastern Cherokees had begun to master the symbols, slowly spreading literacy throughout the tribe.

Water Snake championed the new learning, arguing that it offered opportunities for the Cherokees to consolidate their hold over their homelands in Georgia. "If our people had access to a written language, the many villages could be better informed of the actions taken by the tribal council," he argued, "and we could develop more effective strategies to protect our homeland from the Americans. If our people were literate, we could circulate newspapers or books among the villages, informing tribal members of government policies which affect them."

"I'm not so sure," Westbrook answered. "If we develop our own written language, won't we become less like our fathers and more like the white man? Won't the spread of such literacy undermine our traditional Cherokee ways? Would it not be better if we secluded ourselves within our mountains and refused the Americans permission to enter our lands? Perhaps if we withdrew unto ourselves and refused to acknowledge the Americans' presence, they will ignore us and let us continue as we have in the past."

"Brother," Water Snake replied, "my heart wishes to accept your answer, but my head warns me that you are mistaken. We can no longer ignore the Americans, for their numbers increase and they stand poised upon our boundaries, eager to overrun us. It is no longer possible for us to declare war upon them and to drive them from our villages as we did in the past. Moreover, we cannot close our eyes and wish for them to vanish. Our only choice," he continued, "is to make ourselves strong with those weapons the Americans respect, political unity and wealth. If we can muster these weapons, we may be able to save our lands for our children."

Then, knocking the ashes from his corn-cob pipe into the fireplace, Water Snake added sadly, "even with the literacy we may not be able to withstand their greed. But if we remain uninformed and disorganized, we surely shall lose our homelands."

* * * * * * *

Throughout American history, but especially within the twentieth century, there has been a tendency for both Indian people and especially their white neighbors to associate "Indianess" with the past. Fostered in part by anthropologists, many of whom were eager to investigate what they described as "traditional Indian culture," untainted by white contact, the concept of such an Indian world, "pure and unchanged since time immemorial" has emerged as part of the popular concept about the history of tribal people. Indeed, today many Indian people look back upon their forefathers of the past two centuries as living in a golden age, when they existed apart from the nefarious influences of the whites, a time in which they followed a lifestyle which had made few changes through the centuries.

Such thinking probably fosters a rightful pride in one's tribal past, but it also possesses some inherent dangers. As the two vignettes at the beginning of this essay attempt to illustrate, Indian people have always been faced with change. Antelope and Wolf-That-Follows may have disagreed over their tribe's decision to adopt horses, but since the animals ultimately proved so useful, the Kiowas and other Plains tribes eventually incorporated the animals into their way of life, eventually evolving into the rich culture that dominated the Great Plains during much of the nineteenth century. And of course the Cherokees were unable to hold onto their homelands in Georgia, but their adoption of Sequoyah's alphabet may have strengthened their fight to remain in the East. Most certainly, it enabled them to retain much of their rich tribal heritage. Undoubtedly, the adoption of horses by the Kiowas, and the alphabet by the Cherokees did not make either people less "Indian."

The experiences of the Kiowas, Cherokees, and other adaptive Indian people through the centuries offers some important perspectives to Indian people in the twentieth century. Today, as in the past, the remaining Indian homelands (the reservations) are threatened by outside interests eager to exploit their resources. In the past, such exploitation has regularly occurred as Indian lands were overrun by white economic interests. In fact, most of the reservations that have persisted into the late twentieth century have been those land areas which whites originally deemed undesirable. Most of the reservations containing good agricultural land have been allotted and have passed out of Indian hands. The rich farm land of eastern Kansas and Oklahoma now belong to whites. The Navajo Reservation in the Four Corners region, or the Sioux lands in the Dakotas possess a stark beauty that endears them to their owners, but whites generally have assessed these lands as undesirable.

In recent decades this assessment has changed. Modern demands for increased energy resources have focused upon reservation lands in the West. Black Mesa in northeastern Arizona may have a limited agricultural value, but its coal potential has made it a target for economic development. Other coal and mineral deposits on Indian lands have come under similar siege, and the battle for western water rights has just been initiated. As most economists agree, the key to continued western development is water, and in many western states the tribes' legal rights to utilize critical water supplies has been challenged. Indeed, the fight over finite supplies of water in the western states probably poses the greatest threat to any natural resource now under Indian control.

Any viable historical perspective of Indian-white relations over the past two centuries does not give much cause for optimism. In the past, when Indian people have held natural resources desired by mainstream America, those resources have been taken. To assume that modern Indian communities can effectively deny outsiders any access to these resources is naive. In addition, to assume that the federal government will consistently protect tribal assets from private exploitation is to ignore the government's past record. The economy and government of the United States is controlled by powerful economic interests, and government officials traditionally have been heavily influenced by those interests. If the American public believes that it needs the energy resources available on Indian reservations, those resources probably will be exploited, despite protests by Indian people.

If such exploitation occurs, which seems more than probable, the task of the reservation communities is to maximize their control over the development of these resources, and to minimize the destructive impact of such development upon both the Indian land base and the tribal communities. To maintain such control, these communities must develop the technological expertise to manage their own resources; they must develop a cadre of people with the skills needed to maintain Indian hegemony over the development. There is a desperate need for Indian geologists, mining engineers, business managers, and even accountants. The tribes need skilled laborers, computer operators, and support personnel who can provide those key services needed to keep the development in Indian hands. They also need highly trained attorneys and investment counselors to protect the legal rights of the tribal entities and to insure that income generated from resource development is put to good use.

Colleges, universities, and other institutions of higher learning have a critical role in this process. It is imperative that they provide young Indian men and women with the skills needed to develop and protect these resources. Indian Studies Programs can play a critical role in coordinating such activities and in providing the support services to facilitate the students' transition from the reservation communities to the institutions of higher learning. Indian students should also be encouraged to enroll and major in such traditional academic fields such as geology, engineering, accounting, and business management – fields which will provide the students with the technical expertise needed to manage tribal resources. In addition, these students should be encouraged to do their best to excell in such programs. College programs or departments that do not require high academic standards for their Indian students foster a world of false security. They not only cheat the students, in the long run they deprive the tribal communities of a desperately needed skilled leadership.

Yet can young people leave the reservations, acquire these skills, and return to reassume their place in the tribal communities? Will the acquisition of this training, as some of its detractors claim, preclude highly trained young Indians from being accepted back into their tribe? Will they become "less Indian" because they have obtained the technical expertise available from institutions of higher education?

Such assertions reflect the naivete of their authors. Most tribal experiences have never been characterized by such static, unchanging "etched-in-stone" cultural patterns. Indian people have always adapted to a changing world. Wolf-That-Follows may have refused to acknowledge such change and may have continued to painstakingly follow the buffalo herds on foot, but Antelope was far-sighted enough to realize that horses (the new technology) could be used for his people's welfare. Was Antelope, who embraced the new technology "less Indian" because he and his descendants transcended the old pedestrian culture to emerge as part of the rich, mounted hunting life-style of the plains? Of course not. Indian people in the twentieth century also stand at the threshold of important changes. Hopefully they too will ride forward with Antelope, rather than retreat into the past.

Chapter 2

From Indians to Cowboys:
The Country Western Trend

by Donald L. Fixico

A modern-day cowboy holding a bottle of beer ambles across the room of a bar and puts a quarter in the jukebox. He pushes some buttons and Johnny Lee blares out his song, "Cherokee Fiddle." According to the lyrics, "the Indians are dressing up like cowboys put'in leather and feathers on." Have you ever wondered why a Navajo in Arizona dresses like a cowboy? Or why an Oglala Sioux in South Dakota rides a wild bronc in a rodeo, emulating the cowboy who helped win the West from the Red Man and who was the traditional enemy of his ancestors and their ways? It seems ironic that Indians have exchanged much of their traditional garb for that of the cowboy. But many have and Johnny Lee's lyrics hold true, for much that is identified with the American cowboy is today also associated with the modern American Indian.

Since the beginning of the cowboy period, about 1865, one of the most unusual cultural transitions occurred between the Mississippi River and the Rocky Mountains. Indians began looking more like cowboys than Indians, and this development accelerated with the increased American settlement of the West. Native Americans in the trans-Mississippi West have become immersed in the "cowboy culture" and the country western trend. This development of Indians acting, looking, and dressing like cowboys persists today and mirrors a common social movement of many Americans to emulate the cowboy culture. Indians and whites alike are magnetically attracted to the country western trend.

Today reservation Indians in the western states habitually wear cowboy hats, leather boots, and other trappings of the American cowboys. They wear western shirts of bright print patterns with snap buttons tucked into Wranglers or Levis. The jeans are held up by a thick leather belt with a large silver, turquoise buckle. Their jeans cover up the tops of the Tony Llama, Justin, or Nacone boots which are beautifully stitched with intricate designs.

The current trend for Indians living west of the Mississippi is driving a pickup, wearing cowboy garb, and listening to country and western music. This adoption of cowboy characteristics is interesting and ironic.

Native Americans, who were physically suppressed after decades of wars on the Plains, Plateaus, and Southwestern deserts, have since dressed like their conquerors.

The American Indians' adoption of styles other than their traditional dress exemplifies the evolution of Native American cultures. Basically, Indians are practical and adaptive. Even before the first white man set foot in the western hemisphere, the original inhabitants adopted cultural items from each other. Many items and customs were introduced to tribes through war, trade, and other forms of contacts. Indians coming into contact with other tribes started new linguistic dialects. Groups from different geographic areas traded for highly valued items such as tipi poles, shells, metal items, and later, horses. Such items were often integrated into native cultures.

In comparison with white Americans, who emphasized creativity and innovation, Indians appeared less advanced – according to white American standards. More time and energy were devoted to developing art, religion, and the psychology of dealing with one's self in the Indian world. "Mother Earth" supplied all for the two-legged and the four-legged. Conversely, white Americans sought to utilize natural resources in huge quantities, destroying the natural environment. Differences between Indian and white cultures show vast dissimilarities in viewpoints. Indians are more tolerant, accepting their way of life and seem passive in general, whereas white Americans continually change their lifestyle and appear impatient. But this is not to say that Indian Americans refuse change; rather they change when an improvement on their way of living is called for. Cultural items, more utilitarian than their own, were borrowed. A classic example was the white man's iron cookware, replacing baskets, pottery, and animal skin pouches.

The adoption of the horse was the most revolutionary change among the Indians, influencing romantic equestrian images for Indians and whites – the "Plains Warrior," "Cowboy," and "Pony Soldier." After the Indian wars on the Plains, reservation life and acculturation undermined the image of the nomadic Plains warrior. Whereas the role of the horse as a part of Plains Indian life-style began to erode, the steed remained a de facto characteristic of the cowboy country and western image.

Yet, why have American Indians dispensed with native clothing to dress like cowboys, and why do they continue to do so? Practicality is the most logical explanation. This phenomenon of transculturation in the West can be traced to the early nineteenth century when contacts occurred between American pioneers and Indians from different western tribes. The Turner thesis, which explains the birth of western Americana on the frontier, can also be somewhat applied to the Indians on the Plains and in the Southwest. The Turner thesis hypothesized that American pioneers introduced eastern United States and European cultural characteristics to the West, although many alteration of Old World ways had to be changed to suit the rugged environmental conditions. Likewise, Indians simultaneously adopted American cultural characteristics which were incorporated into their culture. At the same time Manifest Destiny acted as a catalyst in accelerating cultural transmission. Rapid American expansion in the West produced an ever-growing white population whose material culture influenced the Indian tribes.

Even more, the end of the Civil War marked the beginning of a new era in American culture. Reconstruction and empire building in the West encouraged white settlement and ushered in the cowboy culture. Seemingly, for every Indian dressed in buckskin and feathers, there were at least two and three times as many cowboys wearing calico shirts, jeans or overalls, hats, and boots. Mere domination of the Anglo-American population in numbers over the Indians during the cowboy period, from roughly 1865 to 1890, transformed the appearance of the majority culture from Indian to cowboy.

Following the military defeats, Indians experienced pressures to imitate the dominant culture. The federal goverment encouraged transculturation of Indians. Federal Indian policy called for a system of reservations and allotments for the assimilation and acculturation of Indians who were forced to imitate white Americans and to end traditional practices associated with their native customs. Instead, reservation life demoralized many Indians leading them to question their cultural ways and mode of dress. This was a critical period of subjugation and forced assimilation. Ethnocentrism of Western Americana convinced many Indians that their native cultures were inferior to the American cowboy culture, causing Indians to gravitate toward the dominate culture.

In retrospect of the cultural history of the West, the cowboy image has overshadowed the Plains Indian warrior image. In fact, the cowboy image is currently a faddish part of western civilization from Switzerland to San Francisco. Its popularity is increasing, attracting Americans to the cowboy country and western trend. Many people are unaware of their cultural heritage, since American culture is young in comparison with European and other world cultures. Left without deep cultural roots, Americans often experience an identity crisis and do not realize this is happening to them. Typical blue-eyed Americans may be part French, Irish, Swedish, and Dutch; yet, they know very little about Gallic traditions, Irish history, Dutch customs, or the Swedish language. Wandering as "free spirits" looking for keys to their past to satisfy their lonely ego's lost cultural identity, they seek their roots. This cultural void causes many Americans to become obsessed with learning about their past. Many identify with recent fads, especially those with an historical context. In this way they satisfy their curiosity and fulfill a psychological need to learn about their ancestral past, some seeking their roots aboard the **Mayflower.**

American Indians possess a longevity of diverse cultural heritages. Their generations of families and kinship link the people to their past, preventing a need to seek their cultural roots. Their association with the cowboy and western trend is one of cultural borrowing, rather than a personal desire for identity satisfaction.

Finding one's "roots" for many Americans has been temporarily obscured by the cowboy country and western scene, a social phenomenon currently sweeping the West and urban areas across the country. Commercials, media, songs, and images persuade people to believe that the cowboy image, emanating primarily from Texas, is highly representative of American culture. Houston, the nation's fastest growing city, reflects the growing popular cowboy country and western interest; its oil industry is a major contributing part, adding a contemporary touch. Dallas is not far behind as another one of the fastest growing areas and has connected with Fort Worth to become a Metropolis of Texas. Dallas is also the site and name of a popular night-time television series. And recently a new day-time soap opera, entitled "Texas" was put into production and another series, "Concrete Cowboys," made its debut.

In retrospect, the West seems romantic and appealing. Television shows and films have increased the popularity of things country and western. "Honeysuckle Rose" and "Urban Cowboy" have amplified the trend, portraying a fantasy that appeals to many Americans. Understandably, the pressures and anxieties of American life have enhanced the success of the social trend. The macho image of the cowboy and his rudimentary charisma of manliness is envied and has attracted the attention of Europeans. Every American is confronted with the cowboy image in some way, even if one finds it repugnant. Frequently the country and western trend is criticized, but sometimes we unconsciously tap our foot to a Waylon Jenning's song. Many Americans identify with the cowboy image by wearing cowboy hats and boots, driving pickups, and listening to Willie Nelson and other popular country and western singers. This is no less true to American Indians than it is with the rest of American citizens.

Assimilated Native Americans in most parts of the west experience a similar cultural void as that of other Americans. The mixed-bloods and full-bloods, who have been raised without prior knowledge of their Indianness, have little experience of their native culture. A substantial number of Indians have been adopted or placed in boarding schools where they are raised to young adulthood with very little knowledge of their native cultures. In addition, some Indians have chosen to forego their cultural past to live as mainstream citizens in society. Later they sometimes desire to learn about their native past. Over the years these individuals experience personality differences or an identity crisis resulting from our fast-paced, stressed, neurotic society. In this sense, these Native Americans are no different than white Americans or other ethnic Americans who are without a cultural identity. Basically, people need a cultural past which they find comforting. During a national or world crisis they especially need a cultural identity for security and stability. They need to know where their people came from and which traditions they must defend. In brief, identification with a cultural past enables people to escape from tension and establish a base from which to operate against social threats.

In contrast, Indians, who are raised in their traditional ways do not experience this cultural identity crisis like other Americans. Their tribal cultures are soundly intact, highly visible, and still evolving. Their situation isolates them from the mainstream society. Yet, they seek to find a balance between their native culture and Anglo culture, while co-existing in the white man's society. Interestingly, American society and the federal government are convinced that traditional Indians on reservations and in rural areas have social and psychological problems, compounded by economic hardship and poor health conditions. High rates of suicide and alcoholism are cited as evidence, but actually the problems resulted from the pressures of the dominant society on Indian community life. This presumption is erroneous without realizing that Indians enjoy reflecting upon their native past and practice traditional customs daily. Their Indianness disallows the loss of cultural identity, and it seems shocking that they appear more content than the rest of American society. For this reason, western Indians can comfortably wear the same style clothes as cowboys without feeling that they are purposely replacing their Indian identity.

Obviously traditional Indians are concerned with providing for their families, but they have learned to accept the circumstances and fulfill only the basic needs from available sources. Man's needs are not as great, and Indians believe they can live with less. World and national crises do not occupy the noble mind of the traditional Indian. His attention is on his family, on his job, and probably, on the next rodeo, powwow or sing. He will drive his late model pickup to these events, symbolizing the encompassing growth of the cowboy country and western trend.

Ford Broncos and Chevy Blazers are popular for handling the rugged terrain on reservation roads where four-wheel drive vehicles or at least a pickup is mandatory. The hard environments of reservations dictates the lifestyle in Indian country, as it did during the pioneer settlement of the trans-Mississippi area. Solutions to make life easier stressed practicality, and the Indian strategy for dealing with the rocky, dry, and frequently dusty American West has been the pickup truck.

For practical reasons, the cowboy hat became another popular cultural item with Indians. The ten-gallon hat and other varieties of hat-wear from the cowboy era provided protection from the sun and dust. Hats provided better protection than war bonnets from the sun and dust, but they also attract attention. Indians have an eye for outstanding apparel, and cowboy hats are most fashionable. "And don't we have to keep in style?" In this sense, Indians are like the rest of society. The style of the hat band reflects fashion and cultural change. The exchange of a head band for a turquoise, feather, or beaded hat band well indicates the transculturation of Indians today.

Cowboys boots represent another cultural item that has been readily adopted. Boots are designed for riding first and the high tops to protect legs from brush and snakes. But they are not always comfortable to walk in for distances. Practically speaking, boots are more suitable for the rugged western terrain. They last longer than moccasins, and their tough leather covering provides better protection for the calves of the legs. Boots are replacing moccasins, except on some reservations, where elders prefer the latter. In addition, jeans have replaced buckskin, used most often today for pow wows and ceremonies. Buying jeans and other clothes is much easier than preparing leather for clothing.

Western belts have become a natural part of the cowboy country and western style. Often leather strippings, lace belts, and a name ingrained on the belt indicates the rightful owner. The style of the buckle is often silver and large. Such an outstanding part of the entire wearing apparel suggests certain characteristics, exemplifying the cowboy image – strength, dominance, and machismo.

In spite of the dominance of the cowboy image, Indian cultural items in dress have gained recent popularity. The Chicago **Sun-Times** reported in 1980 that fashions in Paris included Indian pins, necklaces, hat bands, and feather belts. Deerskin jackets, calfskin vests, ceremonial shirts, and especially moccasins were in popular demand. On the west coast, the Los Angeles **Times** advertized Indian fashions. In a turnabout, the mainstream society was culturally borrowing Indian items to wear. This fad lasted briefly. People were more prone to hero-worship cowboys who exacted an unrealistic, idealistic image.

An explanation for the charismatic appeal and popularity of the cowboy country and western trend is the magnitude of its imagery. An attractive image of the West is projected that encompasses a history that is romanticized, including a leisurely style of western dress and a slow vernacular that can be easily imitated. A style of western music and the western swing, two-step, and other dances encourages people to act like cowboys. The media has created heroes of the West who are envied and idolized – Randoph Scott, Gene Autry, Roy Rogers, and John Wayne. Thus, a style of dress enables us to step into the past, to escape our anxieties and become like the cowboy. People can escape reality and return to the "happy-go-lucky" day of the Old West where virtue, justice, and freedom reigned supreme. All of these elements constitute the success of the trend, allowing all Americans to enjoy a different culture.

Finally, an explanation for the current growing cowboy country and western trend lies in observing the last two decades. Social rebellions characterized the 1960s with a counter-culture dominated by a hippy generation. Flower power, civil rights movements, rock and roll music, and miniskirts exemplified symptoms of a discontented American society that enthusiastically responded to reforming social conditions. Even the previous decade of the 1950s had a well-defined culture of the Republican Eisenhowerism, conservative attitudes, patriotism, and a middle-class society. During this score of years, Native Americans attempted to revitalize their Indian identity, especially during the 1960s, trying to re-capture some elements of the country and western trend.

But the 1970s were different. As the United States entered an economic recession and moved closer to its Bicentennial, Americans seemed at a loss – culturally. Hard rock, acid rock music, and drug cults were signs of a neurotic society of unstable youths who were bombarded with all kinds of new theories to answer the social and psychological ills of time. American confidence, a strength of the nation, wavered; optimism began to disappear. If there was a consistent descriptive characteristic of the 1970s, it was its constant inconsistency. Pessimism prevailed and this uneasy feeling has carried over into the 1980s. This uneasiness enabled Americans to attach themselves to cultural groups that had roots.

People continue to search for their past for strength, stability, and peace of mind. Seeking alternatives sometimes, Americans have taken up a wide spectrum of hobbies and many are unusual. As quickly as fads are created, Americans take them up, but they are not satisfying enough. The cowboy image of country and western culture is fulfilling the social and psychological needs for many Americans, at least for the present. Interestingly, the glamorous sunny lifestyle of California and the bright city lifestyle of New York are being challenged for the limelight of national attention by the magnetic cowboy country and western lifestyle of Texas. Everyone has the urge at sometime to don a cowboy hat, and for somewhat different reasons, Indians are acting like cowboys, too.

Chapter 3

The Twentieth Century Horse:
The Role of the Pickup Truck in Indian Country

by Clifford E. Trafzer

During a formal presentation to college students at Window Rock, Arizona, a professor asserted that Navajo culture had changed dramatically as a result of contact with the Hispanic population of New Mexico. The professor then asked the Navajo students to list the things their people had acquired from the Spaniards. The students considered the question but said nothing. The professor then suggested that one thing the Navajos had received from their contact with the **Nakai** was associated with transportation, adding that all of the students were very familiar with this "thing" that had so changed Navajo society. The students carefully reconsidered the question, before one student quietly but seriously said, "the pickup." Others agreed, nodding their heads before one student explained that the New Mexicans from Albuquerque, Gallup, and Farmington had contributed greatly to Navajo culture. They had introduced the pickup truck.

The Navajo students were not too far adrift. The pickup is the horse of the 20th century, and few elements of technology, if any, are as important today to Navajos and other reservation Indians as the pickup truck. Indians from rural areas, particularly young Indian students, have grown up with pickups which serve their communities in so many different ways. Chevrolets, GMCs, Fords, and Dodges comprised the bulk of the trucks found on the reservations. But like the larger American society, an increased number of smaller trucks – Toyotas, Nissans, Isuzus, and Couriers – have made their appearance on Indian reservations in recent years. Both two- and four-wheel drive pickups are found on reservations, but usually four-wheel drive vehicles are preferred because of their ability to tread through mud, snow, water, and ice. During extreme winter weather, like that of January and February, 1985, four-wheel drive trucks are the only trucks that can possibly move through the Southwestern reservations.

The major disadvantage of the four-wheel drives, however, is the higher gasoline consumption of these vehicles. Indians nationwide have a low per capita income, especially on reservations where most jobs are blue collar. The jobs usually pay little due to large numbers of unemployed people who vie for the few existing jobs. Thus, in the decision to buy a two-or four-wheel drive truck, Indians on the nation's reservations must consider the purchase price of the vehicle as well as the high price of gasoline at stations, stores, and trading posts. The price of gasoline on Indian reservations is generally higher – usually ranging from .20 to .50 cents per gallon more than that found off the reservations. In part this is caused by the fact that most reservations and Indian lands are located in rural areas. Gasoline must be specially hauled from the busy routes of commerce onto the reservations, where road systems are poor and inadequate for heavy truck travel.

Most new pickups purchased by Indians are bought off the reservations. Unfortunately, few truck dealerships exist on the reservations, and where such dealerships exist, they are usually owned by non-Indians who can afford to establish such expensive businesses. Most trucks purchased are new, because dealerships often lend money on long-term plans (but at high interest rates) which Indians can afford. Bank loans are more difficult for reservation Indians to obtain, and large sums of cash are not available. For these reasons, most Indians buy new vehicles which have the added attraction of not having been "driven till their tail's a'draggin'." Most trucks are purchased in border towns surrounding the reservations such as Gallup, New Mexico, Yakima, Washington, and Rapid City, South Dakota. Through the years, this phenomenon has caused a tremendous financial drain from the reservation to the border towns. Indians constitute some of the nation's poorest people, and the flow of money from the reservations to the border towns significantly harms the reservation economies, inadvertently placing a financial burden on every Indian living there. This is particularly important in light of the racial tensions between Indians and whites in the border towns, where the vast majority of the businesses are owned by non-Indians who provide goods and services – including trucks, parts and services – for the reservation populations.

Indians not only purchase their vehicles in the border towns, but they also buy their groceries, lumber, hardware, and a wide variety of dry goods in these communities. Pickups are used to transport the people into towns where Indians purchase their goods. Trucks provide Indian families with transportation to and from border towns which amounts to social, cultural, and economic contact with the outside world. Transportation is a necessity to buy the goods needed for daily survival. In addition, trucks serve Indians with transportation to centers of entertainment, including movies, restaurants, and shopping. Most reservations lack extensive entertainment centers or shopping centers, and therefore Indians travel to border towns where they can find such services. Furthermore, governmental offices, and quality medical facilities are found off the reservations, so Indians must travel to the towns and cities to reach these facilities. And since their main mode of transportation is the pickup, they use this vehicle as the twentieth century horse. Pickups have become such an integral part of reservation life that many tribal governments purchase pickups for official tribal use rather than automobiles.

Indians often use their trucks as their principle means of transportation to important business and professional meetings. Business trips for their tribes – including meetings with state, local, and county officials – are conducted in pickups. They travel to meetings of the National Congress of American Indians, state, national, and regional Indian Education Associations, Tribal Chairmen's Association meetings, and a host of other regional gatherings. Furthermore, individuals travel to border towns for business and banking as well as for religious and social reasons. Many Indians travel to churches (Native and Christian) and religious events. They drive to and from such events as Pow Wows and a panorama of different ceremonies on and off their reservations.

Sporting events have always been a part of American Indian culture. Today Indians travel long distances to participate or view sporting events, including football, basketball, and baseball. Yet one of the most popular sports among American Indians is rodeo. And wherever a rodeo is held, pickups abound. Like their horses in the past, the trucks appear in every conceivable shape and form. Some show their age and use; others look as though they will soon appear in a television commercial. Paint in a wide range of colors and designs grace the twentieth century horses. Like clean, well-groomed horses of old, pickups parked at a rodeo represent wealth and status. Feathers often hang from rear-view mirrors, and in ceremonies like the Navajo Enemy Way, feathers decorate the body of the trucks (horses were formerly decorated with feathers). Bumper stickers announcing, "Your in Indian Country" or "I'm Indian and Proud of It," appear on the bumpers and offer a new form of decoration. Indians use their decorated trucks to travel across the nation to rodeos, but they also transport their horses which they use for calf roping, bulldogging, barrel riding, and team roping. Historically, horses have been an integral part of certain Indian tribes since the seventeenth and eighteenth centuries. Today they remain an essential element within many Indian communities, but they are no longer as important as pickup trucks.

Besides rodeos, horses are used by Indians as a means of transportation, exchange, and leisure. Indians haul their horses with their pickups from town to town and state to state, just as they transport their hogs, cattle, and sheep. Indeed, livestock is an important part of the economic well being of many Indians, who use their pickups to move their ranch stock to markets, pastures, and fairs. Pickups are also used today in cattle and sheep drives, where long distances are covered without the use of large trucks or railroad stock cars. In these cases, pickups become chuck wagons, carrying supplies, food, and equipment. Significantly, trucks serve as bases of communication through their citizens band radios and their AM-FM stereos. In the evening, ranch hands gather around their pickups to listen to cassette and eight-track tapes of Willie Nelson, Waylon Jennings, and Ricky Skaggs. Pickups have taken on this added characteristic in recent years, since communication and entertainment are important elements in American Indian culture today.

Indians living in rural areas also supplement their incomes by raising produce. Crops are sold in nearby towns or along the busy highways bordering their lands. Some Indians market their produce in make-shift fruit and vegetable stands, while others simply sell their harvest from the beds of their pickups. Corn, wheat, melons, squash, pinon nuts, and many other foods are sold in this manner, and the principal means of moving their produce is via pickup trucks. This is true not only of foodstuffs but of Indian arts and crafts which are sold to tourists visiting Indian country. Moccasins, paintings, drums, rugs, blankets, jewelry, and the like are sold out of pickups on or near Indian lands. Many people set up household in their pickups while selling their goods, living in campers and shells attached to their trucks for short periods of time.

Pickups are also important through their use in hauling water, wood, and fuel. Since reservations are often located in remote regions of the country–lands which Indians have occupied for hundreds, sometimes thousands of years–the lands are sometimes void of water and must be hauled into these areas from far off rivers and lakes, wells and springs. In pickups, water is transported in large metal barrels. Some Indians, fortunate enough to have sufficient money, have their own water wagons and pull them behind their pickups. All life depends on water, and the very survival of many Indians depends on water being moved by pickup trucks for use by humans, crops, and livestock. Water means life to family members, ensuring also the survival of the extended American Indian community, including elders, the infirmed, and those unable to purchase a truck of their own.

Fuel sources of wood and coal are important as well, providing warmth, light, and cooking. Wood and coal are often found on Indian reservations, particularly those located in the far West. Yet the fuel is not always found near a person's home, so wood and coal are usually hauled several miles in pickups. This is an important function of trucks, and one which is also tied to the physical survival of many Indians who would perish from the cold without fuel for their stoves. This was graphically illustrated in the winter of 1984-1985 when Navajos and Hopis died from the extreme cold. Snows, winds, and mud prevented the delivery of fuel to families living in remote corners of their respective reservations. Some Indians rely on electricity, natural gas, and propane to heat their homes, but many Hopis, Navajos, and others depend solely upon the natural gifts of the earth surrounding their homes. Sometimes fuel resources are transported great distances, and Indians sometimes miss school and work to haul wood and coal for their families.

Moving anything in vehicles across most Indian reservations is a difficult task owing to poor road systems. Because of the lack of money to construct roads, many arteries of transportation on reservations are little more than trails, cut by the tires of trucks rolling across old foot and horse paths. The deep imprint of parallel tire ruts run in every direction across the earth in Indian country. These ruts form the basis of most roads found there, and constitute the most common road system found on reservations. Like an intricate pattern of lines found on an elder's face, tire tracks run endlessly through Indian country. Indeed, on the nation's largest reservation, the Navajo, over 5,000 miles of road criss-cross the plateaus, deserts, and mountains. Of these, less than 1,500 miles are paved and all of the roads are simple two lane thoroughfares, almost all of which have been paved in the last twenty years. Because of the large number of unpaved or unimproved roads found on the reservations, trucks, not cars are the most efficient means of transportation in the rural lands owned by Indians.

During the past two decades, many tribal councils have established their own programs to improve roads, bridges, and culverts. Sometimes tribes have been able to work with county and state officials to construct and maintain roads. Too often, however, state and county governments are most interested in improving roads through Indian lands that benefit the non-Indian population, rather than building and maintaining roads that would specifically aid Indian citizens. Government officials often argue that overseeing these roads is not their duty, sometimes claiming that Indians pay no county or state taxes and therefore should not receive the benefit of public road projects. Of course, Indians pay taxes, but they usually do not have the political clout to influence policy decisions. Despite such problems, however, roads have been graded, graveled, and paved on Indian lands. And many road conditions have improved in recent years, but they are far from being as well developed as those found in the non- Indian communities surrounding Indian lands. Since road systems are so poor, Indians rely heavily on their trucks.

Because of the difficulties posed by weather conditions, trucks are used as tools in Indian country. Mud and snow plague much of the region in the winter and spring, and pickups are used to tow equipment, wagons, and other pickups. Broad metal blades are attached to pickups, and the trucks are used to plow snow and remove mud from roads. During other seasons, the blades are used to grade roads, level the ground for new buildings, and clear brush. Winches are often attached to trucks and used to drag snags, pull stumps, and stretch fences. A very adaptable people, Indians ingeniously use the wheels of their pickups to generate power to saw logs and operate pumps. Native Americans have learned many ways to use their vehicles and keep them operating.

Since auto service centers did not exist on many reservations until recently, there has emerged on Indian lands a distinct cultural phenomenon –the cult of the "Indian mechanic." Men and women alike have become legendary for their feats in mechanical engineering. With the use of bailing wire, tin cans, and black electrical tape, Indians have been known to repair their trucks and keep them running effectively for years. This is impressive considering that they often keep their pickups rolling with the use of only a few modern tools, including crescent wrenches, ball-peine hammers, pliers, and screwdrivers. With these choice tools and a good measure of common knowledge, Indians keep their trucks operating through every season of the year.

Unquestionably, pickup trucks have become a part of Indian culture and society today. Men and women alike make use of the trucks throughout the reservations, and they attach a good deal of importance to their vehicles. Before pickups were introduced to Indians, horses were one of the great symbols of wealth and status. Indians bragged about their horses and placed bets on their mounts, since gambling was a part of American Indian life. Horses remain an important component of many Indian societies today, but much of the social emphasis formerly placed on one's horses has now been transferred to the pickup. Trucks have become the modern status symbol to many Indians who compare their pickups with those owned by others. They use their trucks for transportation of people, livestock, and produce. They operate businesses from their pickups, and use them as collateral in business transactions. Trucks are used to move heavy items, to plow snow, and to cut wood. They are important to the very survival of many Indians who depend on the vehicles to haul wood, water, and food. But they are also status symbols among Indians.

Thus, in so many different ways, pickups have become a part of the American Indian way. Humorous stories have developed around the pickup truck, like the one involving a white man who was asked by an Indian to see if the emergency lights worked on a pickup. The white man reportedly stood at the rear of the truck studying the taillights for some time. Losing patience the Indian seated in the driver's seat rolled down his window and called out to the white man, saying "well, are they on or not?" The Anglo responded, "well, now they are, now they're not, now they are..." Trucks have become such a part of American Indian life that they are today a part of the oral tradition.

Pickups have become a part of the social fabric of American Indian life today in many ways, including the material culture. Trucks can even be seen in the beautiful pictorial rugs of Navajo people. In recent years pickups have been woven into Navajo rugs and appear in settings filled with mountains, deserts, hogans, sheep, and horses. Furthermore, silver buckles, beaded hat bands, and oil paintings depict the interrelationship of the twentieth-century Indian with pickup trucks. Unquestionably, pickups are important in the larger society of rural America, from Illinois to Idaho and Alabama to Arizona. But this is especially true in Indian country, where pickup trucks are often the most important element of modern technology. Pickups have become as much a part of the rich culture of the American Indian as the bow, canoe, and snow shoe. It has been adopted and adapted to the rural life of many Indians, and it serves numerous American Indian communities all across North America. Like their ancestors who proudly rode their painted horses, modern Indians drive their pickups across their homelands. Thus, to many Indians north of the Rio Grande, pickup trucks have become the horse of the twentieth century.

Chapter 4

The Comanche Shield:
Symbol of Identity

by Christopher H. Bentley

While visiting a friend, the author became intrigued with an Indian shield hanging on the right side of the fireplace. The author had seen it many times before, but on this occasion he asked questions concerning its origin, age, history, and significance. After a lengthly discussion with the owner, the author became convinced that this shield was not just an art object but an historical piece of material culture that could explain a portion of Plains Indian culture. The author determined that much could be learned about the Indians who made and used this piece. This idea became a challenge, resulting in a thorough examination. For the Plains Indians, the shield had great cultural value, and this shield in particular held a special fascination because it was of an unfamiliar tribal style. Many questions were raised about the shield. Was the shield used in ceremony or in war? Which of the many Plains Indians had made it? How was it made, and from what era was it constructed? Were there any rights or responsibilities associated with owning a shield of this type? Shields were initially used to deflect club blows, spear thrusts, and oncoming arrows. Sometimes shields were even able to turn musket balls. With the advent of repeating rifles, the shield lost is protective value in a physical sense, and from then on offered protection in a supernatural sense, becoming more of a protective amulet. Some questions soon emerged, particularly regarding the shield's construction and decoration. What materials were needed and used? What was involved in decorating a shield? These and other questions developed while examining the physical features of the shield.

The shield consists of a shield proper and a drape. The shield proper is of a circular, convex shaped piece of rawhide, approximately 44 cm in diameter. The face of the shield is elaborately painted. The central design is a cross or four winds motif in red, extending about 8.5 cm from each edge. In each quarter, created by the cross, is a yellow triangle with the addition of small boxes at the base, possibly representing stylized bear paws. Each of these triangles has its base directed toward the shield's edge. The background is green. The edge is painted red, forming a circle, which encloses the central designs.

The drape is made of buckskin and is attached in a way so as not to cover the shield's face, hanging over the top and along the sides forming a horseshoe shape. The bottom part of the "trailer" is also of buckskin in a trapazoid shape extending downward a total of 86 cm from the shield. An interesting feature of the drape is that it is entirely outlined in tin cones. As with the shield face, the drape, too, is painted. The paint, however, is softer and has faded with time. The upper part of the drape is red, augmenting shield paint by giving the illusion that it is part of the shield proper and not the drape. The bottom of the drape is also painted. The part closest to the shield is a faded green. At 6 cm the green is terminated by a black line running horizontally across the buckskin; below this line the hide is painted red. Just below the black line is a strip of bead work 12.5 cm in length, directly below the beadwork and following its entirety are tin cones.

The shield is made not of one, but of two pieces of rawhide. The space between the two rawhide pieces is filled with some undetermined material, averaging 1.2 to 2.0 cm thick. The two pieces are laced together around the outer edge with rawhide lacing. The lacing holes were punched with an awl, rather than burned. On the backside of the shield, pencil marks are found along the outer edge. These may have been put there to help the maker achieve his desired shape. Also, on the backside of the shield a few small patches of hair remain, and they do not appear to be buffalo. This is confirmed by an existing brand mark found on the back of the shield's outer edge. The rawhide used then is not bison, but either horse or cow. On the shield's face are four pairs of holes, one pair in each quarter, burned through the hide. Through these holes pass buckskin thongs which are attached to the "arm ties." This attachment also holds the shield drape in place. The thongs were run through the holes before the shield was painted. This is easily determined by moving the thongs and seeing the places that were devoid of paint.

The shield paint consists of a mixture of vegetable or native paints and trade paints. The red encircling the edge is a type of red ochre made from crushed iron oxide or red earth, while the red used in the four winds motif is a type of trade vermillion. The four winds motif is entirely outlined in black ink. The yellow ochre that fills each triangle could be derived from several different substances, including yellow earth, pine moss, or crushed buffalo gall stones. The medium blue that outlines each triangle and each small rectangle at its base is a common trade paint. Trade paints involve no preparation, except the addition of water and hide glue. The background is a pale green, native in orgin and made from green algae.

The buckskin drape that covers the shield is made in three sections. To see the construction, the back of the shield has to be viewed. The first or central part of the drape is a round piece of buckskin approximately the shield's circumference. A horseshoe shaped piece fits over the top and hangs along the shield face. A trapezoid piece is connected to the bottom. All pieces are attached with a buckskin thong, as opposed to sinew. The entire drape is secured to the shield by the ties that also bind the arm straps. On the painted side of the shield, none of the drape construction techniques are visible. As mentioned above, the drape is painted on the front, but not on the reverse side.

Two additional points of interest concerning the drape are the tin cones and the beadwork, both of which indicate white contact. The tin cones are homemade and of three different sizes: 6.4 cm on the horseshoe piece and the trapezoid trailer; 3.4 cm on the bottom of the horseshoe tabs; and 1.6 cm below the beadwork. The 390 tin cones that outline the shield and the trapezoid section are individually cut inward at the open end of the cone. The other two sizes are flat across the open section. They are all attached to the drape with buckskin thong. Each thong has two cones which pass through a hole across 1.2 cm of the leather, then out of the other hole on the same side. A knot in each end of the thong drawn into the cones prevents them from falling off. This method allows for an equal distance of thong between drape and tin cone. The cones swing freely and produce a tinkling noise when the shield is moved. The different size cones produce different tones, all of which are pleasing to the ear. This added characteristic provides this shield with a musical balance. The tincones beneath the beaded strip are attached on a seperate piece of leather which is sinew sewn to the drape. The beaded strip is done in three colors of 4/O Italian seed beads. The design is a simple banded pattern 1.2 cm wide done in pony trader blue, translucent navy blue, and sky blue. The beaded strip is done with sinew in the typical split-stitch fashion, common to all Plains tribes. The beadwork was done by a woman and not a man.

The last details of the shield are the arm and shoulder ties. The armstraps consist of parallel buckskin strips secured by thongs running through the holes in the shield face and knotted on the back side. The shoulder strap is also of buckskin and is attached to each arm strap with a simple knot.

The construction technique of the entire shield and the extensive use of tin cones helps identify the tribal origin of the shield. Tin cones were often used on the Southern Plains, and the number of cones indicates that the shield was more than likely made there, rather than on the Northern Plains. Furthermore, an examination of the ethnographies of Plains tribes suggests that only one tribe constructed the double-layered shield. That tribe was the Comanche which once inhabited parts of present-day Texas, Oklahoma, New Mexico, and Kansas.

Traditionally the Comanche made shields from the shoulder hide of an old buffalo, as this was believed by these people to be the toughest part of the hide. While the hide was still "green," the hide was staked out, hair side up, over a pit containing a small, hot fire or heated rocks. Water was added to the fire and the resultant steam began the process of shrinking and condensing the hide. While the hide was still hot, scrapers were used to remove the hair and flesh. The process was repeated as many times as necessary to achieve the correct thickness. At this point, the maker cut out the two circular pieces required for the shield. Holes or eyelets were punched around the outer edge, and a small stone was used to eliminate wrinkles. The two pieces were laced together, and the space between the two was filled with hair, feathers, grass, or paper. The well known Texas cattleman, Charles Goodnight, related that a Comanche shield he once procured was stuffed with the pages of a complete history of Rome. The padding was placed between the two layers of rawhide and laced together while it was still pliable. The convexed rawhide was then hung up to dry. The shrunken rawhide pieces could also be laid over a slight mound to dry. Once dry, four pair of holes, one pair in each quarter, were burned through the shield face with a hot poker. The shield was allowed to dry to a flint-like hardness, but before decoration occurred, the shield was tested. The shield was hanged from a tree branch and used as a target. At a distance of approximately fifty yards, the shield maker fired arrows at the shield. If any of the arrows penetrated the shield, the piece was discarded. If, however, none of the arrows pierced the shield, it was decorated.

Many Comanche shields were left plain, but those that were painted and decorated were done so in a prescribed manner. Strict rules governed the decoration of a shield, because, as Ernest Wallace pointed out, the painted shields usually had power and the designs symbolized that power. A Comanche had three ways to procure or create a shield with power. The warrior could find a man who already owned a medicine shield which had power and could request that some of the "medicine" be transferred to his shield. Second, the warrior could seek a vision with the hope that a "spirit source" would instruct him in a powerful design. The third method was to ask a medicine man to procure the medicine design for him.

If a warrior chose the first method, he visited the owner of a medicine shield, taking with him a pipe filled with tobacco. When the pipe had been completely smoked, the request was made. Having smoked together, the medicine shield owner rarely refused the request. If the owner did not wish to grant the request, he simply refused to smoke with the visitor. This behavior, however, was considered anti-social and selfish. Most often, the medicine shield owner agreed to help and would do so by actually painting the warrior's new shield as a duplicate of his own. Although he gave away some of his power, the original medicine shield's power did not diminish.

The second method is dream inspired. The man sought a vision on a spiritual quest or during sleep. In either event, the spirit dictated the design to the warrior, and in turn the warrior dictated the design to an experienced artist who painted it on the shield. The third method was for the warrior to request the help of the medicine man. After prayer, the medicine man gave the warrior instructions including the procurement of an artist to paint what the medicine man dictated. If the owner wished to understand the design, he was to take the shield to an isolated spot and ask the shield to explain itself.

For their services, the warrior paid the people involved in giving the shield its power. Payment was in the form of horses, other items of material wealth, or both. Medicine painting was something not taken lightly, and the desire to have a shield painted was a reflection of a warrior's status, his ability to secure help from the proper individuals, and the ability to pay for their services.

Most Comanche shields were made with shield covers or drapes, including the one under examination. The shield cover fits completely over the shield face. A drawing thong is found on the back of the shield which tightens the leather and prevents the cover from falling. Additional paints and decorations were affixed to the shield cover. Decorations included feathers, bear parts, scalps, and horsehair. These decorations brought more power to the shield and served as a type of billboard statement about the owner. According to Comanche tradition, the painting or application of bear parts indicated that the warrior was an exceptional hunter. Scalps indicated the prowess of the man in warfare. Horsehair or horsetails indicated that the warrior was exceptional at raiding. Feathers or hair, which fluttered in the wind, were added to the shield to disturb the aim of the enemy.

The shield drape was more common among Southern Plains people, and it was decorated in the same manner as the shield cover. The use of the drape had an added benefit. When the shield was in use, the leather on the back side of the shield protected the arm from being rubbed raw against the shield proper. Sometimes, the combination of shield cover and shield drape were used by Comanches. The drape in this instance did not fit over the back of the shield, but instead was attached to the shield cover. The drape was often made of trade cloth, including the trailer section, and both were sinew sewn to the shield cover. It was not uncommon to find shields with more than one shield cover, and in most instances, all of the covers were painted in different manners. The Comanches believed that such a shield had great power.

Physical strength and spiritual protection were necessary to ensure a warrior's safety in battle. Painting and decorations produced spiritual protection against the onslaught of an attacking enemy. Indeed, shields were not simply display or ceremonial items. They were used in the heat of battle. A Comanche warrior was trained to deflect oncoming objects – arrows and musket balls. The shield was not held stationary. It was moved high and low, as necessary to prevent injury. To practice this, Comanche warriors became living targets, as their friends fired arrows, while the warrior skillfully deflected them with his shield. Friends shot arrows without points at their comrade, who had to move quickly to prevent being hit. The bumps and bruises received in practice served as a constant reminder to keep the shield ready in battle. After rifles were introduced on the Plains, Comanche warriors carried shields into battle to receive the spiritual power which they offered. This power alone was believed by some to be sufficient to protect the warrior. This medicine power of the shield remained even after the shield no longer deflected projectiles.

After the Red River Wars and during the reservation era, the Comanche shield was still produced and used. Shields then had a broader protective quality in a spiritual, not just a military, sense. A warrior made his shield according to tradition and followed the regulations governing its use. But instead of carrying it in war, it was carried in ceremonies, dances, and parades. The shield changed, since Comanches made lighter ones for dances and ceremonials, no longer needing the heavier war shields. The shield took on a new meaning, since the shield protected the owner and his family from new enemies: starvation, disease, and acculturation.

During the reservation era, the Comanche warrior continued to abide by specific regulations. The shield never touched the ground, and when it was not in use, it was kept in a buckskin bag. It was not kept inside the lodge but had to be hidden in a tree some distance from camp so that it was never near water, grease (e.g. cooking utensils), or menstrating women. The shield's power was lost if it had such contact, and the owner was injured as a result of this violation. On his trek to get his shield, a warrior rode in a half circle to the shield's location. Once it was retrieved, the warrior moved back to camp in a circular path. Having completed a full circle, the warrior was able to receive the benefits of the life-giving sun. A powerful medicine shield could never be given away but was thrown into a stream with a swift current so as to wash away the power. Most shields ended up in the creek. Very few were ever given away.

The shield specimen previously described was made from cow or horse hide, not buffalo hide, which was not available to the maker. Most likely, it was made during the early reservation era. Since the hide had been branded, the rawhide used to construct this particular shield came from either the hind quarter or the front shoulder, since branding in the 1880s in the Indian Territory was permitted in both of these areas. The paint used in decorating the shield came from two sources, native and trade paints.

The artist who painted this particular shield used both native and trade paints, combining both traditional and contemporary materials. The design itself, consisting of a four winds motif and four stylized bear paws, was chosen by the maker. However, no interpretation of the design can be made, since only the maker could explain the shield's meaning.

The drape was made of either deer or antelope hide which indicates that some game was still available. Game was not always plentiful, however, and hunting off the reservation was often a necessity for survival. Although this drape was made from game animals, Comanches usually did not carry shields when they hunted game. The beaded strip on the shield drape is unusual but indicates that it was done by an old woman. Comanche tradition has it that after menopause, women were considered physiologically the same as men. This accounts for beadwork on a medicine shield which was surely done by an elderly woman. Tin cones are another unusual form of decoration on a medicine shield, although two other examples of their use are known to exist. One is a Comanche shield in the Paul Dyck Foundation and Research Institution of American Indian Culture. It also has a drape outlined in tin cones, and the tin cones run in two horizontal rows on the trailer. The shield is believed to be circa 1850. The other example is a photograph taken by Cannery in 1892 of a Kiowa named White Horse, holding a shield with a drape outlined in tin cones. This not only shows that tin cones were used on shields but also gives some parameters in dating the specimen outlined here. The shield under examination was made between 1875 and 1885. It is a medicine shield and not a "grass shield" or plain, undecorated shield. This is a shield that was used in ceremonies and parades, but not in dances because the shield weighs 2.5 kg, far too heavy an object to carry long by a dancer.

The shield is in excellent condition, because it probably was never used in war. Furthermore, the shield was never thrown into a stream, since there is no water damage. And since Comanches rarely sold or traded shields, it is likely that a non-Indian found it, the shield was sold to Fred Harvey and Company. At a Harvey House along the tracks of the Santa Fe Railroad, the shield was stored or displayed until an eastern writer, Irving S. Cobb, purchased it. After many years in his collection, the shield was bought by the actor Leo Carillo, who added it to his personal collection. There the shield remained until Carillo's estate was sold. An unidentified buyer, purchased the shield which was then sold to Hubert Guy, in whose collection the shield remains today. He bought the shield believing it to be of Kiowa or Apache origin. However, after reviewing the evidence provided here, Guy feels that it is Comanche.

Each piece of Plains Indian material culture is unique, providing a story which adds a great deal to the understanding of Plains Indian culture and history. More important to the Comanches, this shield offers an object of cultural continuity which provides a focus of identity. The shield holds special meaning because of its tie to the past. Many elements of American Indian identity exist today, including objects like this shield. The shield is a part of the larger cultural fabric of the Comanche Indians. It is more than a piece of art, it is an object of history, one which tells us much about one of the great tribes who inhabited the Southern Plains.

Chapter 5

The Road to
Middle Class Indian America

by Michelene Fixico

George Thundercloud glanced up at the clock and noted that it was nearly 1:00 p.m. It had been a busy Friday morning in the Indian CETA counseling office, but his calendar had deliberately been kept clear for the rest of the afternoon. George picked up his briefcase, waved goodbye to his coworkers, and walked out to his car. He drove to the urban Indian health center to pick up his wife, Cathy, who was employed there as a bookkeeper. By the time they reached their house, their two children were already home from school. Everyone quickly changed into casual clothes and began loading the car with suitcases containing outfits for fancy dancing, a tent, and their camping equipment. The excitement was noticeable. George's eldest son was competing for the first time at a powwow. Although the powwow was only 85 miles from the city, the Thunderclouds knew that for the next 48 hours their jobs, school, and middle class lifestyle would be forgotten as they immersed themselves into the Indian world of the powwow.

The Thunderclouds are representative of a growing middle class Indian America. According to the last United States census, over one half of the American Indian population now lives in urban areas. As more of the Indian population shifts from rural communities to cities, and as tribes expand economic development programs on reservations, more Indian families will reach middle-income levels. The question arises as to whether the Thunderclouds of the 1980s will also adopt those middle class values which were the bane of young people in the 1960s and 1970s at the cost of their tribal values.

American youth of the 1960s are now in their thirties and forties. Most have families of their own and are earning mid-level incomes. Ironically, many have settled into the very lifestyles they had protested against, while others have had to make compromises. Middle class Indian America can be summarily categorized among those who have made compromises. They are middle-class, but as Indians they still retain much of their traditional values. This retention can be attributed to the struggles they faced on their journey towards middle-class status, unlike their white counterparts who had been raised in middle-class families.

The unique historical, political, and social experiences of Indian people led them to their middle-class status. For two hundred years the American government and Christian organizations have been trying to assimilate Indians into mainstream society. Everything conceivable was tried, from reservations to land allotments, from the Bureau of Indian Affairs (BIA) and mission schools which shunned and ridiculed Indian culture and language, to short-lived programs aimed at revitalizing cultures, culminating in the disastrous urban relocation and federal-Indian trust termination programs of the 1950s and 1960s.

In the nineteenth century federal officials and Indian supporters felt that alloting land to individuals would force Indian people to turn to agriculture and education to sustain themselves. Once the tribal land base was destroyed, hunting lifestyles would no longer be possible, thereby destroying tribal communal traditions and culture. Government officials believed that Indian people would eventually become a part of the mainstream society. The same type of reasoning was proffered for removing children from their homes and placing them in Bureau of Indian Affairs and mission schools for extended periods of time. Separation from their families and friends meant they would not be able to learn their languages and cultures. The termination and relocation programs of the 1950s and 1960s were also an effort at making Indians a part of the "melting pot." The end result of these efforts, however, was extreme poverty and disease on reservations and the creation of Indian ghettos in the cities.

The experiences gained by Indian people during the height of relocation and termination facilitated the growth of a middle-class Indian America. Many Indians gained expertise and knowledge in dealing with state and federal bureaucracies during their struggles with the government's termination policy and relocation program. They began to realize the importance of formal education in putting Indians on a competitive basis with white America. Indian leaders spoke of the need for Indian lawyers to protect the rights of the people, doctors to serve in Indian communities, and educators and administrators to direct local governments and programs. Indian youth were encouraged to continue their education to serve as role models for their younger siblings and to obtain the "book" knowledge that could be used to help their people. As record numbers of young Indians entered colleges and universities in the 1960s, they became very aware of the inequities in American society. Indian people learned from the protest movements of other groups, especially the civil rights movement. This can be seen in the actions of the American Indian Movement (AIM). As Indian youth experienced the heights of emotion generated by the activism of the sixties, they directed their energies toward the needs of the Indian community through protests, marches, and occupations – the same methods utilized by young people of all races throughout the country.

Indian people were aware of, and in some cases, part of the protest movements of the 1960s and 1970s. A closer examination of this period, however, shows that Indians were actually engaged in a separate, but parallel protest. The escalation of the Vietnam War under President Lyndon Johnson and the explosion of the civil rights movement of the 1960s fomented the social unrest which pervaded this country. The first publicized expression of white middle-class discontent, however, can be attributed to the protests at the University of California-Berkeley in 1964. Herein is the first major difference between the white middle-class and the Indian movements of the 1960s and 1970s. For American Indians their first protest action to receive widespread publicity was the occupation of Alcatraz Island in 1969, five years after the first Berkeley protests. The Berkeley protests signaled a growing concern with national politics, bureaucratic control, and education. The Indians on Alcatraz were trying to publicize the economic and social plight of Indian people. Both groups utilized protests and sit-ins; both were dissatisfied with government policies and education; but they were concerned with different issues within that broad scope.

The fear generated by the Vietnam War and dissatisfaction with federal policies soon led to concerns of world destruction. As young Americans became more aware of shrinking natural resources and the ramifications of continued racial inequities, they became more doom oriented. They began to turn away from anything that represented the "establishment," the older generation who was responsible for the policies of this country. Young, white middle-class Americans increasingly became disenchanted with the class conscious values of society and the impersonal pervasiveness of government bureaucracies. They rejected the materialistic values of their parents and turned to communal ideologies and drugs in search of a utopian society.

Young American Indians also protested against the dominant society's middle-class values and bureaucracies, but from a different perspective. While white youth raged against world hunger and injustices, Indian youth protested against the poverty, disease, and despair prevalent on reservations. While both groups found fault with the American government's handling of the Vietnam War, Indian youth also pointed to the failure of the government to meet past treaty obligations. Indian youth were also quite familiar with the shortcomings of the government – they had years of experience with the Bureau of Indian Affairs. Both Indians and whites were caught up in the emotions of the protest era. Each group reacted in the same way, but to different issues. This difference between white middle-class and American Indian concerns can best be discerned by examining college campuses during this period. Extracurricular activities, lifestyles, clothes, and music illustrate the similarity in actions and the differences in motivational factors.

Pan-hellenic organizations experienced a decline in popularity during the 1960s and 1970s. Many college students felt the organizations perpetuated the artificial middle-class values they professed to reject. They felt that members of these organizations were more interested in maintaining a false status quo and values, rather than finding solutions to important world problems. Indian students also expressed disdain for fraternities and sororities, or for that matter, any club or organization. They also felt that social groups perpetuated elitism. For Indian people, their concerns went further. Elitism contributed to class structures, and the end result was continued prejudice toward a group of economically depressed people who had refused to become mainstreamed. More importantly, these organizations were more concerned with social activities than the existing problems of poverty and disease in their own backyards. Indian students were trying to regain their culture and find answers to problems on the reservations. They did not have the time or energy to waste on perceived superfluous activities. Some Indian students joined Native American clubs, however, which gave them an opportunity to share ideas, revitalize tribal cultures, and learn about traditional beliefs, and to keep abreast of current Indian activities.

The clothing of this period was a symbol of young people's individualism and a rejection of styles that could identify them as middle class. In addition to the ever present beads, they wore faded bluejeans with patches and teeshirts (the ultimate extreme being the fashions of the early 1970s when stores sold prewashed patched bluejeans). To round out the picture of independence from their parent's values, some students rejected monetary aid, choosing rather to live in low-cost housing and support themselves with low-paying jobs. For most Indian students, they did not have the luxury of being able to turn away from money, nice homes, and clothing. The luxuries were simply not there for them to reject. Indian students were coming from economically depressed reservations and low income Indian communities. Fortunately for these young Indian people, who were very familiar with hardships, their clothes and housing accommodations fit right into the college campus scene of that era.

The idealism of youth was manifested in the music of the sixties and seventies. While young people everywhere listened to the anti-establishment ballads of Joan Baez and Bob Dylan, Indian youths also listened to the protest songs of Floyd Westerman, Buffy St. Marie, and XIT. While the former were being hypnotized by songs of peace, brotherly love, and equality, Indian youth were encouraged to return to their tribal communities and beliefs, to maintain their "Indianness," and to be proud of their heritage. While others listened to futuristic songs predicting "big brother's" control and impending doom, young Indians were emotionally stirred by songs lamenting the conditions on reservations and the treatment of Indian people. Indian groups sang about the hope of a growing pan-Indian America and revitalization of Indian culture and lifestyles. Some Indians laughed at the irony of such songs like Eric Burdon and the Animals' "San Franciscan Nights" which professed the "American dream includes Indians too." Others hoped that someday Indians would be a part of the American dream.

There were a few white students who, in hopes of finding that utopian society, turned to American Indian religions and tribal lifestyles in search of themselves. They wanted to get back to nature, to escape the violence and inequities of the world. They hoped to find inner peace and answers to the problems of a technological society. They thought communing with nature, seeking visions through peyote, and cleansing themselves through sweats would give them that peace and the answers they sought. They had no idea what the multitudinous tribal religions were about, and they often tried to carry out ceremonies or lifestyles as depicted in movies like "Billy Jack" or as they imagined them to be from the little information they gained from anthropology classes and the popular "Indian" books of that period, such as Carlos Costeneda's TEACHINGS OF DON JUAN.

For Indian students, the 1960s and 1970s was a period of reawakening. They were consumed with the tasks of revitalizing their cultures, languages, and religions which were the heart of their tribalism. They did not turn to alternative lifestyles, but tried to regain a heritage which the federal government and Christian organizations had attempted to destroy. At the same time these youth had to deal with the perpetuation and exhibition of false images of their cultures which was the result of young whites searching for themselves in ill conceived Indian rituals.

While other college students remained on their local campuses to stage protests and sit-ins against the Vietnam War and bureaucratic policies, Indian protestors left their campuses, traveling to other parts of the country to participate in protests against government violations of treaty rights, the rape of tribal lands by multi-national corporations, and the theft of resources through govermental leases to ranchers and farmers granted by the Bureau of Indian Affairs for very little money. While whites were clashing with state and local riot police on college campuses, Indian youth were facing the might of the United States Coastguard at Alcatraz and United States Marshalls and the Federal Bureau of Investigation (FBI) during the takeover of the Bureau of Indian Affairs Building in 1972 and Wounded Knee in 1973.

Indians from all over the country traveled to Alcatraz to support their fellow Indians, some for the entire occupation, most for a few days. Many more Indians participated in the Trail of Broken Treaties which was organized to protest the treaties which the federal goverment failed to fulfill or recognize. The protest ended in the occupation of the BIA building in Washington, D.C., when promised housing and previously promised meetings with federal officials failed to materialize. The occupation of Wounded Knee in South Dakota began as an investigation into the actions of the tribal chairman on the Pine Ridge Reservation and of the death of Raymond Yellow Thunder. When AIM members reached Wounded Knee, the site of the ruthless massacre of Indians in 1890 by the famed 7th Cavalry, emotions erupted and Wounded Knee became the site of another confrontation between Indians and government forces. According to Vernon Bellacourt, National Field Director for AIM, Wounded Knee happened because diplomatic efforts had failed.

The Indian youth of the 1960s and 1970s were engaged in the protests against middle-class values. But the roots of their protests during that period, centered more on the possible loss of their culture and not the rejection of middle-class values. As Indian people they equated middle-class attainment with loss of culture, breakdown of the extended family, and the forfeiture of Indian values for white middle-class values. Many of those young people who participated in the American Indian protest movement are now a part of a growing Indian middle-class America, and many have become middleclass Americans. They have the position, income, and houses associated with middle-class Americans, but are they the same as white middle-class Americans? Have middle-class Indian Americans adopted those middle-class values which many young people rejected during the protest era? Are Indians guilty of accumulating wealth for wealth's sake, of "keeping up with the Jones," or in this case, "the Thunderclouds"? Have they become part of the establishment?

To answer these questions one must examine the people who now comprise middle-class Indian America. These middle-income Indians came from historically, poverty-striken tribal groups who had been denied those things available to middle-class whites. As young children they experienced the ridicule and shame of poverty at the hands of their white peers. They grew up knowing inadequate sanitation, prevalent diseases – including tuberculosis and middle- ear diseases – malnutrition, crowded and poor housing, and high unemployment. Even as children they were aware that their peers, teachers, and neighbors considered them second-class citizens. As parents, they did not want their children to experience these same feelings and depredations. They saw education as the means of escape from poverty and disease. Material wealth became a symbol of equality, one which the rest of society recognized.

Today's middle-class Indian traveled a long road to reach that middle-income status which on paper made them equal to white Americans. The relocation programs of the 1950s was the beginning of that walk toward middle-class status. During the relocation exodus of the 1950s and 1960s, many Indians left reservations for urban areas in search of jobs and a better way of living. Relocation was a seesaw affair where many relocatees were unable to survive in the cities and returned to the reservations, only to find that they either no longer felt comfortable there or that the economy of the reservation could not support them. Some tried relocation again. They moved to different cities, hoping to make a living for their families. Some never adjusted to the crowded populations, technology, and fast pace of city life. They disappeared into the Indian ghettoes, their families torn apart. Others adjusted to the machinations of city life and employment programs. As they gained more experience in dealing with bureaucracies, they began finding better jobs and increasing their incomes.

Education also played a very important role in the rise of middle-class Indian America. The civil rights movement and the struggles for Indian rights resulted in increased funding for higher education for Indian people. In response to cries for equal opportunity for Indian people, the federal government authorized an unprecedented number of studies on the conditions of American Indians, including the Kennedy Report of 1969. These reports provided shocking statistics on the poverty, inadequate education, and poor health conditions prevalent in Indian communities. Indian people were at the bottom of every category addressed. As a result of these studies and the push for equal opportunity, a plethora of Indian education bills were passed, including the Navajo Community College Act of 1971 and the Indian Self-Determination and Education Assistance Act of 1975. Specialized programs for Indians were funded, including University Year for Action which was designed to allow Indian college students, employed by tribal organizations, to gain college credit for expertise gained on the job. Others included First Americans Tomorrow's Engineers (FATE) for Indian engineering majors and Headlands Indian Health Careers, an orientation program for Indian high school students interested in the medical field. The Bureau of Indian Affairs' additional funding for higher education grants during this period probably had the greatest impact on increasing the number of Indian students enrolled in college.

The results of increased higher education funding for Indian students is very evident today. Some Indians obtained one or two years of college and remained in cities to work. Others obtained bachelors or masters degrees. More important, in terms of earning ability, the number of Indian professionals grew. There are at least 250 Indian lawyers, 30 doctors, 12 dentists, 225 Ph.D.s, and 100 Ed.D.s. Although the number of Indian professionals is small statistically compared to other American minority groups, they are earning salaries, in the mid to upper middle-income range.

They are able to buy homes, televisions, and cars; for the first time they have the resources to open savings accounts and send their children to college.

Middle-class Indian Americans now look and live like middle class America, but they have not forfeited all of their cultural values for those of the middle-class. Indians living in cities maintain their contact with other Indians by working for Indian organizations, albeit an urban Indian organization. They participate in pan-Indian functions including powwows, national meetings, and ceremonies. Indians maintain strong relationships with families and friends, strengthening their own and their children's contact with their heritage. The retention of their cultural roots and values provides them with an identity, something young whites searched for in the 1960s.

Today, middle-class Indian parents ensure that their children learn about and understand their cultures. In large urban areas this can be very difficult. In a study on "American Indian Socialization to Urban Life," conducted by the Native American Research Group in 1975, the researchers pointed out that 92 school children in a study area in San Francisco attended 69 different schools. Although the Indian children were dispersed in schools throughout the cities and had few Indian peers within each setting, they socialized with other Indian children outside the school. Indian parents maintained social contact by traveling to powwows and social events in order to be with other Indian people. They taught their children basic traditional values, including the importance of the extended family and sharing with others.

Indian adults are taking steps to strengthen their own cultural relationships and to insure the maintenance of Indian society and heritage. Some people return to Indian communities to provide needed expertise and services to their tribes. Others are academic professionals, making their mark in colleges and universities throughout the country. They are not only presenting an Indian perspective in classrooms and publications but are encouraging and advising young Indian students. Indians in academics provide expertise on methods by which to preserve Indian history, language, art, and culture. Doctors and lawyers are working in urban and reservation Indian health and legal service programs. No matter what their field or their income level, they maintain ties with the Indian community – the source of their values and culture.

Nowhere is the commitment to Indian values more evident than in the homes. Rather than worrying about "keeping up with the Thunderclouds," parents use their income to attend powwows or ceremonies near and far from home. Instead of accumulating materials of white middle-class wealth, money is spent on dance costumes for children and gifts for giveaways. Many middle-class Indians still retain much of their traditional values which is evidenced by the continued existence and influence of extended families and friendship ties. They always find time to help with fund raisers, to share their expertise with others, and to attend community events. Perhaps nothing more illustrates the attachment to their cultural heritage than the Indians' need to be with other Indians where they can just be themselves.

Middle-class Indian Americans who grew up in the 1960s and 1970s experienced a period of revitalization which greatly influenced their retention of tribal culture and values. Although they were a part of the era of protests, marches, and demonstrations against government policies, world problems, and middle-class values, theirs was a parallel protest. Rather than focusing on world problems or American foreign affairs, Indians concentrated on the problems affecting Indian people. They protested against middle-class values per se, but were actually concerned with the substitution of middle-class values for tribal values. Indian people were not only concerned with improving the economy and health of Indian people, but in developing pride in being Indian.

Indian people fought hard in the 1960s and 1970s for Indian rights, revitalization of tribal cultures and to strengthen pride. Today many middle-class Indians are taking steps to insure that their current lifestyles do not negate those past efforts. They know how allotment, boarding schools, and government policies led to the loss of many tribal songs, dances, and languages. Many remember wishing that their parents had been able to teach them about their culture. They are more determined to teach their own children about their tribal culture. Like the Thunderclouds, many middle-class Indians eagerly look foward to powwows and other Indian events where they can be a part of the Indian world. They earn mid-level incomes and have adapted to middle-class lifestyles, but they still retain much of their culture. They have made compromises in order to free themselves from poverty and discrimination, but they have not forgotten their identity as Indians.

Chapter 6

Tribal Esteem
and the American Indian Historian

by Carol Hampton

"Bloody Fiends," "Savages," "Squaw," "Brutish Barbarians." These are only a few of the terms Euro-Americans have applied to American Indians. Novels and movies depict Indians as "Noble Savages," "Dirty Dogs," and "Lurking Savages," skulking behind trees waiting for a chance to pounce upon some poor, kind, innocent, unsuspecting white person. History books portray the dispossession of Indian homelands in terms of "the clash of a relatively advanced race with savages." Neither novels, historical works, nor popular media have done justice to the study of Native Americans, particularly in light of the oral traditions passed down from generation to generation by tribal elders. Native history relates a different past, one more positive in presentation, and insightful in content.

The contradictory views of American Indians have provided a creative force which has influenced some Indians to study American Indian history and to write on the tribal past. One Native American historian today remembers that as a young girl growing up in Oklahoma City, she took a required class in Oklahoma history. The teacher recognized the unique Indian heritage of the state, but of the sixty-seven tribes domiciled there by the end of the removal period, the teacher mentioned only the Five Civilized Tribes. The historian remembers wishing that the teacher had talked of her tribe, but only the "Civilized Tribes" had been worthy of the teacher's discussion. As a young student, the historian felt unworthy because she "wasn't civilized!"Many tribes have been maligned by grade school teachers, but the Caddos were not sufficiently worthy to be mentioned. History and social studies books totally ignored the Caddos, and as far as the Oklahoma City public school system was concerned, the girl's tribe did not even exist. Years later the girl married a man who was part Choctaw and part Chickasaw–two of the Five Civilized Tribes. The woman reasoned that at least her children had a chance–they were at least half-civilized and thus worthy of mention in their social studies classes, but she resolved to alter the teaching of American Indian history by one day researching and writing her own tribe's history. At least her children would have a record of their Caddo heritage –in addition to their legacy as part of the "civilized" tribes.

Many American Indian historians have come to the discipline of history from a yearning to know more of their own past. Many have a personal desire to add to the body of knowledge by offering oral histories provided by their grandparents and elders. They had recognized a need to fit what they had been taught about American history in school into their knowledge of their own people's history and vice versa. From these beginnings most of them branched out to research and write tribal histories other than their own, examining inter-tribal issues and pan-Indian movements. In many cases this was forced upon them by their own desire to know more, and by friends and students who expected them to know a wide range of American Indian history. They have found similarities in their various tribal histories, legends, and belief systems. They have found differences – some of them profound. Most important, however, they have found errors in the written records, misinterpretations, misunderstandings, and, occasionally, outright fraudulent renderings of the past. They have attempted to expose these problems and to offer a new history which emphasizes an understanding of the American Indian communities as well as white Indian policies.

A popular ethnohistorian with many published books and articles to her credit, once requested certain information for a recent book. The author of this essay willingly supplied the information, expecting that the research material would be helpful and that the writer would use it correctly. But the ethnohistorian had not listened. She had not learned. She changed the author's grandfather's name to Robert, and called him that so many times in her book that everyone who knew him began to doubt that his name really was Frank. This may seem to be a small matter, but a mistake of this sort suggests that similar errors may well abound. And it points to a problem of accuracy found in many histories. The ethnohistorian and other scholars often ignore Indian sources, even when the materials are solicited and provided.

Another kind of misunderstanding, probably caused by a failure to listen, prevails when non-Indian historians write of American Indian heroes – those who have been long revered. Some of these historians write with particular delight, debunking as myth the careers of some Indian leaders. One leader who has suffered this fate more than once is a man honored and respected by most Comanche Indians – Quanah Parker. The term "most" is appropriate, since factions exist among all tribes, including the Comanches. Most Comanches admire Quanah, but others do not. Yet, chapters in two recent studies of American Indian leadership have depicted Quanah Parker as an opportunist – a man only looking out for his own interests. One historian, William T. Hagan, pictured Quanah as rising to leadership only through the aid of non-Indian agents, who picked him for that status because of his non-Indian mother. Hagan debunks Quanah's leadership during the Red River Wars prior to the Comanche arrival on their reservation. And yet, Comanches readily accepted Quanah as one of their leaders. Agents of the Bureau of Indian Affairs could appoint chiefs as often as they liked, but the people accepted those men as leaders or ignored them. Frequently reservation Indians rejected those men selected by whites as leaders, but not Quanah Parker. Comanches accepted Quanah's leadership. Hagan admits, that there is no "persuasive evidence that at any time his rivals really enjoyed more popularity than Quanah among their fellow tribesmen. They might accuse him of selling out to the cattlemen, and make disparaging remarks about his mixed-blood ancestry, but Quanah's stock remained high with most of his fellow tribesmen."

Before this noted historian had admitted that Quanah's fellow Comanches respected him, he made several insulting comments. In reference to Quanah's judgeship, the eminent historian stated: "It was a difficult assignment that paid poorly, only ten dollars a month. However, the status and power inherent in the position appealed to Quanah's ambition to excel, and he cherished the honor." Impugning a man's character by assigning base motives for his actions appears to be a common method used by some historians. Quanah played a well-known role in the leasing of reservation grazing land to Texan cattlemen driving their herds to Dodge City, Kansas. Those cattlemen crossed the reservation, letting their cattle graze as they slowly made their way north, ignoring the admonitions of the federal government against such practices. As Hagan puts it: "Quanah was one of the first Comanche Chiefs to protest these intrusions...However, the cattlemen learned how to appease Quanah and other Comanche chiefs and headmen. Quanah soon appeared on the payroll of the Texans, as did Eschiti and Permansu (Comanche Jack). Primarily they were being paid for their influence...Naturally other Indians resented Quanah, Eschiti, and Permansu deriving income from grazing land that belonged to all. A solution would be to lease land to the cattlemen formally, thus permitting all members of the three tribes to share in the income...Presumably the cattlemen saw Quanah as their most able Indian advocate of leasing, and he seemed happy to play the role. The Texans got an articulate Comanche ally and expressed their gratitude in financial terms to a young Indian trying to live like a white man."

Instances abound in which non-Indian historians have suggested that those American Indians who lived in Anglo-style houses and accepted gifts of money, livestock, and household goods were traitors to their people. Indian leaders have been damned for remaining "blanket Indians" on one hand and damned for accepting values of the dominant society on the other. It almost seems that Euro-Americans want to believe that sometime in the distant past, Native Americans took a common and universal vow of poverty.

Another leader, a man who considered himself Caddo, although he was more Delaware, has been attacked on the same grounds. Nishkuntu was a peyote leader and evangelist. He took the Peyote religion to the Osages, Quapaws, and others. Those people greatly appreciated Nishkuntu bringing the peyote religion to them and recompensed him with presents of considerable value. Today Osages frequently greet Caddos with gladness, mentioning that "your people gave us our religion." And yet the noted anthropologist, V. Petrullo, maintained that: "His enemies claim that in the course of his life he professed to have had fresh visions which always were interpreted to his personal gain." Petrullo stated that Nishkuntu's "followers, in any case, betray their expectancy of financial reward. It was remarked, for example, that the impecunious Seneca gave Anderson, (nephew and follower of Nishkuntu) only his trainfare when he brought peyote to them." Caddos, on the other hand, tell of Nishkuntu and the house he built on his land which he offered to anyone in need. He helped those people who could not care for themselves, giving them food, clothing, and shelter. Non-Indian historians and anthropologists rarely tell this side of the story, but the people do. Listen to them.

Still, books and articles of this sort provide a valuable impetus in the classroom. Uncomplimentary and unflattering remarks about Quanah Parker, Nishkuntu, and other Indian elders almost always lead to lively discussions in American Indian leadership courses taught at University of Oklahoma, University of California, and San Diego State University. Comanches and other Native Americans take exception to such attacks. American Indian historians have a responsibility and commitment to redress such grievances by telling the whole story, both sides of the story. They must explain and analyze the commendable and the corrupt, the self-sacrificing and the self- serving. American Indian historians face twin challenges derived from the fact that they are both the researcher and the researched. They stand directly within a tribal past, and yet as historians, they must stand outside also to be objective scholars. Some have chosen to side-step this problem by researching and writing about tribes other than their own or issues and movements alien to, or at least far removed from, their own tribal identity.

Those who have selected this path sacrifice intimacy for distance, remaining remote from their subjects so as to maintain objectivity. Others have· researched and written their own tribe's history before examining the history of other tribes, issues or movements, far removed from their own past. For some American Indian historians, this has provided a professional balance in their work. In either case American Indian historians should write the definitive works on the tribes and issues without sacrificing objectivity, scholarship, and detail. However, American Indian historians and other Indian scholars have a responsibility to employ the methodologies learned during their formal training to use all sources available – including Indian sources – to produce interpretive studies lacking in the works of non-Indian historians.

Some American Indian scholars prefer to write and speak of what they have learned and know most intimately. It is when they choose to work with issues, movements, and tribal histories close to their hearts – those issues which affect them deeply and personally – that they directly confront the twin responsibilities of objectivity and subjectivity. The question of one's dual commitment to their people, those who have been misunderstood, misrepresented, and maligned and to their discipline is raised each time the scholar begins a project. They bring their own subjectivity to an understanding of their people, and yet they must seek objectivity – the ability to stand aside from a situation and analyze it unemotionally. This task is not an easy one. Formal academic training sets the American Indian scholar apart from most of their fellow tribal historians – those whom the tribe elects or appoints to keep records of their past, whether those records are written, oral, or elements of material culture. Each tribe expects its keeper of the past to uphold and defend it. There is little expectation of objectivity, or desire for it – although tribal historians quickly learn that a certain degree of aloofness is necessary to maintain a balance among opposing factions.

These and other lessons were learned by the author when she began her tenure as Caddo tribal historian. While her research in Caddo history encountered few problems, one clarification became apparent. As a member of the Caddo Tribal Council, she participated in discussions and decisions concerning the tribal seal and flag. To some these matters may seem trivial, but to Caddo people directly involved in internal tribal affairs, these issues frequently created lengthly and acrimonious debates. Such a debate ensued when one of the entries used the name "Hasinai" on the seal. This appellation, "Hasinai" refers only to one, albeit a rather large segment of the Caddo Indian Tribe of Oklahoma, their legal name. The tribe encompasses a number of tribes, villages, and bands – or whatever anthropologists choose to call the tribal groupings – including the numerous groups which had united under a confederacy called "Hasinai." The tribe also includes the equally numerous remnant of the Kadohadacho confederacy – the author's own people.

The tribal seal crisis reached its zenith with a realization, on the part of many tribal members, that they were a long way from unity – even within the Caddo tribe. Only today have tribal members begun to realize that they speak different dialects of a common language because of their unique and separate backgrounds, not because some speak the language incorrectly. The Caddos came together seven generations ago, but they are long- lived people with equally lengthy memories whose oral traditions recall the stories of that union. The elders participated in that alliance when the Kadohadachos were forced out of their homeland and left to wander until their kinsmen, the Hasinai, took them in. The Caddo controversy over the seal and flag ended when the name "Hasinai" was removed. Tempers cooled and a quasi-union prevailed, although one faction of the tribe maintained its identity through a separate dance ground called Hasinai, marking an age-old division within a twentieth century tribe.

As tribal historians, American Indian scholars must maintain some degree of aloofness from their people. As academic historians, they have a commitment to remain objective in their search for the truth. Non-Indian historians of the Native American past frequently argue that American Indian scholars are in search of a "usable" past and that they are not disinterested observers. Objectivity, they assert, remains the sole domain of the non-Indian intellect. Little do they realize that the responsibility to Indian people requires a commitment to scholarly objectivity, not the reverse. Anything less would be a disservice to other Indians and the faith and trust they have placed in their own scholars. And yet, non-Indian historians correctly assess the situation, in that American Indian scholars have a further responsibility to aid Indian people in their struggle to survive in an alien society, a society which denigrates Indians and their traditions, a society which defames Indian heroes and degrades the original inhabitants of this land.

Yes, Native American historians research, write, and teach the prideful past. They have good cause to feel pride in their husbandry of this earth. They have been careful stewards of the bounty of this land. They have much for which to be proud, and yet, non-Indian historians have even tried to rob Indian scholars of this, their intellectual past. The tide is changing, but American Indian scholars must beware. They cannot permit their proud heritage to be denigrated again or cast aside by non-Indian scholars who would claim that American Indian history has no place in our nation's past or simply a secondary one which should be examined by "objective" non-Indian historians who write and speak in absolute "truths."

As Native Americans and as scholars, American Indian historians have a unique position from which to write American Indian history, particularly in regard to access to sources derived from an oral tradition, having heard history first from the lips of their grandparents. The American Indian historians must listen and learn from their elders. The people will talk to them, and they expect their scholars to listen and remember, not with unquestioning minds or zealous hearts, but with open, intelligent minds willing to consider an Indian perspective of past events. Indians know that often when they share their oral traditions with non-Indians, somehow something gets lost. The stories are changed and the meaning misconstrued. Whites do not always listen. Perhaps they already have their own ideas as to why and how an event happened. They want corroboration, not a new perspective. Native American scholars have a responsibility, indeed, a duty to listen carefully. Otherwise, they are as Anglos, and their histories will reflect the age-old bias, rather than offering a new scholarly view.

When the author first began composing papers on native American history for graduate courses, she frequently used the passive voice. University professors warned her to write in the active voice, because passive was dull to read. Later she realized that she had written in the passive because she felt that American Indians during the reservation period and later had been passive at that time. "Things" had been "done to them." They initiated few actions, but had been acted upon. Most Indians passively accepted their fate, but not today. In many ways Indians are once again active politically, socially, and culturally. Indians are in the forefront of historical change through their teaching and writing of their people's past.

Of course, the young scholar learned to write in the active voice, and she learned who had done those "things" to Indians. But she wonders today if that is not basically an Anglo-American, rather than a Native American, viewpoint. That is, writing Indian history from a white, not an Indian perspective. Indians did not know who exactly was "doing them in" during the reservation and allotment eras or just who had authorized the breakdown of traditional tribal governments. All Indians knew was that somewhere lurked a faceless, nameless enemy and that Indians were being "done to." Perhaps, for some periods of American Indian history the passive voice, with its very dullness, carries with it the meaning of a profound truth. Writing from an American Indian perspective and following the dictates of formal academic training while also listening to the Indian elders, does not make the American Indian scholar immune from pitfalls. The author's research and writing on the Native American Church illuminates a problem that American Indians, involved with their own people, occasionally face. No topic is more controversial than American Indian religions, for to write about religions is to write of the sacred–the very essence of American Indian communities.

Don Chaino was chairman of the Oklahoma Conference of Native American Churches when he visited a class at the University of Oklahoma on American Indian history. In an earlier newspaper interview he had stated that he thought officials of the Native American Church needed to discuss their religion with non-Indians in order to educate and enlighten the local "vigilantes" so as to stop continued harassment. On the basis of this article, the instructor invited Chaino to address the class. In the course of that lecture, he stated that when the Native American Church wanted their story known, its members would write it themselves. He discussed no part of the sacred aspects of the religion, its beliefs, or its rituals. Clearly, the time had not yet arrived for him to divulge that pertinent information. The professor teaching the course respected his judgment.

After the class ended, Chaino seemed somewhat disturbed. He knew that the professor was writing articles on the Native American Church, but he did not know what aspect of the Church she discussed in the works. Within a week a fellow tribal council member and leader of the Caddo Native American Church told the professor that Don Chaino had met him on a street in Chaino and told him that he should keep a tighter rein on the author. The Caddo leader defended the professor and her work, pointing out that she was a member of the Caddo Tribal Council and a member of the Caddo Native American Church. The message was clear. The professor could be trusted!

But the problem remained. The author's own tribal leaders told her that they trusted her to treat with respect that knowledge she possessed. Personally, she found it extremely difficult to proceed with her writings on the Native American Church. She well realized that white scholars, like Omer C. Stewart, Weston LaBarre, and James Slotkin–all noted, non-Indian anthropologists and ethnohistorians–could write and publish details of sacred matters. They could divulge information given them in trust. But the author refused to betray the trust her people had placed in her. If she continued to study and write about the Native American Church, she had to find a way to do so without offending members of that religion, including herself.

As a scholar and an Indian, the author chose to leave all discussion of ritual and speculation on holy mysteries to anthropologists and ethnohistorians. She confined herself to the legal history, opposition and current status of the Native American Church and to the importance of that religion in contemporary American Indian life. She felt that the growing harassment endured by peyotists had parallels not only with other American Indian religions, but with the rights of many religious and ethnic minorities whose practices are sufficiently different from those of the dominant society. These parallels suggest that Native American historians have a unique opportunity to contribute and offer new perspectives in comprehending American history in general and American Indian history in particular. Indeed, the trials experienced by American Indian scholars might well serve as a model for a better understanding of all historical experiences.

Chapter 7

America's First Discipline:
American Indian Studies

by Carter Blue Clark

Before 1492, actually prior to the Norse landings in 1000 or so, American Indian Studies exclusively dealt only with American Indian peoples. American Indian Studies encompassed all of native life, being responsible for infant training, child rearing, camp upbringing for youth, and higher education for shamanism, the priesthood, or other more specialized teaching within clans, societies, and traditions. Indian Studies served to train people as farmers, hunters, clanmothers, traders, warriors, orators, fishers, holy ones, elders, and many more. Family, clan, and traditions carried the individual Indian forward into a fulfilling and complementary life within the village and tribe. Before the coming of Europeans, Indian people successfully educated their own. Indian Studies was confined to American Indians.

The Norse were the first historic Europeans to colonize North America, establishing a series of small Viking outposts. Many were timber-cutting and wintering stations, ranging from Iceland, along the coast of Greenland, and at least some were built along the northern Newfoundland coast of North America. Calling the mainland natives "Skraelings" (for "pygmies, weaklings, barbarians"), the Norse came and went for perhaps as long as 400 years (980? 1350?), maybe even longer, without making a permanent, large-scale impact. The Norse did not participate to any extent in American Indian Studies, except as observers. Relations with the natives, whether Eskimos of Greenland and northern Canada or Beothuk and Micmac Indians of the Newfoundland region, deteriorated in direct proportion to the frequency of the Norse visits and the length of their stay. Eventually, the Norse in Newfoundland fell prey to Indians, the elements, or starvation. They left the region forever, becoming the vanishing white man.

Longer continuous contact between Europeans and indigenous peoples of the North American continent occurred following the Spanish entradas of the sixteenth century into the Southeast and the Southwest, and the French and English excursions into the Northeast. Along the New England coast, the initial American Indian Studies instruction took place with whalers and fishers who were wintering or drying their catch. Among the earliest known Indians to serve as an American Indian Studies instructor to the English colonists, Squanto stands out as the best known. The isolated and suffering Pilgrims of Plymouth along the Massachusetts coast survived in large measure as a result of Squanto's efforts. Squanto's course in American Indian Studies taught the Pilgrims to survive by catching and storing fish, planting new food crops – corn, pumpkin, beans, squash – and mastering other aspects of woodcraft necessary to the continuation of their toehold in the new land. From his side, prestige derived from the foreigners helped Squanto in his relations with other Indians. There was some give and take, at least at first.

Either through capture, shipwreck, or as a result of running away from the early European settlements, whites in small numbers joined the Indians. Gradually the ranks of Indian Studies grew. More and more European and African colonists came and remained. They, too, wanted to know how to survive and prosper in America. Economic and cultural motives led Europeans to focus on wealth and to concentrate on how to use the natural riches of America. The Indians instructed the whites and shared their knowledge, even when initial generosity toward newcomers turned to hostility. American Indian Studies was no longer restricted to Indian peoples. Non-Indians in a very real way gave rise to the discipline. Admittedly, only a very few non-Indians cared to learn more than relatively rudimentary information about the American Indians who were gradually being pushed away from or swallowed up by European settlements. The few Europeans who pursued studies of Indians included an occasional local dilettante or quack, a missionary who yearned to convert the "heathen," and a fur trapper who shunned his neighbors in the developing towns and sought winter wives among Indians. All of this activity really began the first American Indian Studies.

The indigenous people did not single themselves out for scrutiny and examination. There was no formal course of study that led to a Bachelor of Science degree with a major in hunting and a minor in cultural arts, such as dancing. There was no formal course of study, because it was unnecessary. The Indians had no need for a distinct Indian Studies, for the cultural elements of the natural world provided them representations of their "Indianness" which surrounded them in their everyday lives. The clan symbols and the totem signs were ever-present in the environment and in the stories told as part of their literature. There was no need to define roles or identify cultural traits. Every Indian person was cloaked in Indianness. Before the coming of Europeans, natives were unaware that they were "Indian" at all. Christopher Columbus penned the label for the natives, and it stuck.

From the outset, the European colonists pressured Indians to alter their lives and change their ways. Missionaries were the most visible agents of European change. All other segments of colonial societies pushed Indians to make themselves over in the European image. Educational, religious, and economic endeavors sought to take the "Indian" out of the individual native and to replace that with European colonial, later American national, traits. Whether in New England praying towns, Paraguayan reductions, or California mission communities, the ultimate goal was native metamorphosis. Many of the American Indian converts to the various enterprises undertaken for them left the white world and returned to their Indian traditions. When the Indians departed, they took with them metal objects, a horse, a gun, or other Euro-American manufactured goods or concepts. The white world touched Indians in many ways, some seen and some unseen. Much was added to American Indian Culture, for Indians were an adaptive, pragmatic people. Their world irrevocably changed.

The dominance, independence, and separateness of Indians gave way to a subordinate status within the United States under the successive onslaughts of manifest destiny. Alien cultures surrounded Indians, engulfed them in new societies and kidnapped them for boarding school deliveries. Within the alien schools, Indians were forbidden to speak their native languages and had their mouths rinsed with soap for so doing. School officials forced the children to have their long hair cut and their clothing burned. With chopped hair and store-bought clothing, Indian children were made ready to enter non-Indian homes, far away from their relations, in order to learn domestic, civilized skills. Policies confined freedom-loving tribespeople to reservations, then those reservations were diminished further into a remnant through allotment, sales, and fraud. Forced assimilation took a tragic toll among the lives and spirits of indigenous peoples.

The assimilationist pressures did not fully succeed. A small revival of Indian cultural heritage and arts occurred under the Indian New Deal of the 1930s, which helped lay the foundation for the rise of Red Power and the renewal of Indian nationalism in the 1960s. World Wars, policy changes, termination, economic development programs, and self-determination desires fed demands for Indian control over native lives. Within education, the arrival of a new awakening in things Indian increased interest in American Indian Studies. The discipline had changed, just as native peoples had changed. American Indian Studies no longer exclusively dealt only with Indians. Classes began and students filed into their seats, all kinds of students – not just Indians. That presented a paradox. American Indian Studies strives to participate in the university environment and seeks academic respectability from its peers. It is ironic that Indian Studies strives on the one hand to find acceptance by borrowing the very values that Indians have so often opposed and found repugnant. Staff in American Indian Studies must build upon the very acculturation aspects that Indian people have found so difficult for so long. American Indian Studies is trapped in that irony.

Adopting a story from Roger Buffalohead, for a long time involved in Native American programs, the dilemma facing American Indian Studies is best illustrated through a parable involving an airplane. A wealthy Indian purchased a plane and hired a white pilot, making very sure that the pilot knew that the Indian owned the airplane and was the boss. One day the Indian owner decided to "Indianize" his plane. He fired the white man and hired an American Indian to be the pilot. The Indian hired was not without flying experience – he had watched planes fly in Korea and had been on board several during the war. But he had never before flown an airplane. The American Indian pilot flew the plane into a mountain on the first excursion. Both died instantly. On his way to Indian Heaven, amid the distant and nearing sounds of the feathered choir that awaited the Indian owner of the plane, he turned over in his mind what went wrong. He analyzed the circumstances surrounding his demise, seeking to know where to place the blame. At first he thought it was his fault. Next, he determined it was the pilot's fault. At last he found what he knew was the answer and realized the solution to the entire problem – it should have been an Indian-made plane!

The problem for the wealthy Indian did not originate with the mechanics of the operation, but with the non-Indian corruption in manufacturing. The plane owner assumed that but for the non-Indian adulteration, he would still have been aloft. It did not occur to him that the cause of his woe might reside outside his limited perspective. American Indian Studies is trapped in the same cultural dilemma. Ethnic studies cannot easily be slotted within a traditional campus department. American Indian Studies fits no standard academic mold. American Indian Studies is by its nature interdisciplinary. Indian Studies borrows from music for its songs, takes from botany its plant ecology, lifts from history its background analyses, joins with theater arts for its dances, builds upon comparative literature for its prose and poetry. Indian Studies contributed to the interdisciplinary nature by the fact that Indian Studies does not have a single home in any one of the traditional disciplines.

By its very nature American Indian Studies is not mainstream within higher education. American Indians are unique, and so is their discipline. They stand alone among all of the other ethnic groups because of their history, which involves treaties, tribalism, and other aspects that set them apart. Not being in the mainstream of higher education is both an advantage and a disadvantage. It is an advantage because Indian Studies can rightly stand separate from other academic programs, just as Indian students tend to remain aloof from other ethnics. It is a disadvantage because Indian Studies is vulnerable in its isolation.

American Indian Studies does not always behave like the mainstream in higher education. Indian students require counseling and guidance on a college campus to assist them in adjusting to the larger society and its demands for competitiveness. Aggressive competitiveness and individuality stand in stark contrast to most American Indian cultures that teach the norm of behavior is to submerge the individual within the group. Another reason American Indian Studies does not act like a mainstream department in all of its aspects is that Indians are not whites. Indian faculty may not carry all of the cultural baggage that denotes mainstream society. Indians as faculty have different pulls on their time and resources that non-Indian faculty do not have.

Community concerns are a factor in American Indian Studies faculty retention and promotion that often are not taken into sufficient consideration by university administrations. In spite of unique circumstance, tenure decisions are frequently made on the basis of mainstream faculty activities that preclude many Indian Studies faculty needs. Conversely, many Indians look upon American Indian Studies from their community perspective with the same eyes as the wealthy Indian owner of the plane, lacking clear insights into the nature of the university, ethnic studies and the pulls on faculty time and attention on campus. Sometimes the actions of Indian Studies faculty appear to be going in the wrong direction to community members who do not understand the nature of the academic world which contains its own stresses and requirements for faculty members, Indians and non-Indians alike. New directions for the program, closely watched from the Indian community, may appear unwarranted and antagonistic to the original dictates of American Indian Studies. Yet, changes that have taken place within the university and larger environment may leave no choice to the faculty in American Indian Studies.

The discipline has changed since it first began educating non-Indians and interested Indians in the unique cultural and historical aspects of native societies. American Indian demands for self-determination and for remunerative employment in the marketplace require more course work in mainstream studies and fewer in ethnic studies. Interest in American Indians will continue as a result of the historic legacy of manifest destiny, yearning for family roots, and a lingering romantic attachment to the glories of a bygone era. The necessities of earning a living with marketable skills will not lessen the need to maintain Indian cultural ties and to learn more about one's Indianness through American Indian Studies. Even though some of the attributes of Indian Studies will alter with changing demands from society and administrators, American Indian Studies will continue to offer insights into America's most unique cultural heritage. The basic mission of American Indian Studies is to enlighten and educate all students about the diverse and rich cultures that make up American Indian life. For Indian Studies to continue to fulfill that function, it will take understanding on the part of faculty, students, and community members who have a common interest in the education of all students in the ever-changing world of the American Indian.